Praying The Lectionary

Prayers Of The Church for Worship

Cycle B

Garth Wehrfritz-Hanson

CSS Publishing Company, Inc.
Lima, Ohio

Praying The Lectionary

FIRST EDITION
Copyright © 2020
by CSS Publishing Co., Inc.

The original purchaser may print and photocopy material in this publication for use as it was intended (worship material for worship use; educational material for classroom use; dramatic material for staging or production). No additional permission is required from the publisher for such copying by the original purchaser only. Inquiries should be addressed to: Permissions, CSS Publishing Company, Inc., 5450 N. Dixie Highway, Lima, Ohio 45807.

Scriptures taken from the New Revised Standard Version of the Bible. Copyright 1989 by the Division of Christian Education of the National Council of the Churches of Christ in the USA, Nashville, Thomas Nelson Publishers (c) 1989. Used by permission. All rights reserved.

Library of Congress Cataloging-in-Publication Data:

Names: Wehrfritz-Hanson, Garth, author. Title: Praying the lectionary : prayers of the church for worship : Cycle B / Garth Wehrfritz-Hanson. Description: First edition. | Lima, Ohio : CSS Publishing Company, Inc., 2020. Identifiers: LCCN 2020035648 | ISBN 9780788029660 | ISBN 9780788029677 (ebook) Subjects: LCSH: Church year--Prayers and devotions. | Common lectionary (1992). Year B. Classification: LCC BV30 .W39 2020 | DDC 264/.13--dc23 LC record available at https://lccn.loc.gov/2020035648

For more information about CSS Publishing Company resources, visit our website at www.csspub.com, email us at csr@csspub.com, or call (800) 241-4056.

e-book:
ISBN-13: 978-0-7880-2967-7
ISBN-10: 0-7880-2967-3

ISBN-13: 978-0-7880-2966-0
ISBN-10: 0-7880-2966-5   DIGITIALLY PRINTED

Dedicated to the memory of my grandparents, parents, teachers, and pastors who taught and inspired me to pray.

Contents

Advent 1   15

Lectionary Readings: Isaiah 64:1-9; Psalm 80:1-7, 17-19; 1 Corinthians 1:3-9; Mark 13:24-37

Advent 2   18

Lectionary Readings: Isaiah 40:1-11; Psalm 85:1-2, 8-13; 2 Peter 3:8-15a; Mark 1:1-8

Advent 3   20

Lectionary Readings: Isaiah 61:1-4, 8-11; Psalm 126 or Luke 1:47-55; 1 Thessalonians 5:16-24; John 1:6-8, 19-28

Advent 4   22

Lectionary Readings: 2 Samuel 7:1-11, 16; Psalm 89:1-4, 19-26 or Luke 1:46b-55; Romans 16:25-27; Luke 1:26-38

Christmas Eve or Christmas Day   24

Lectionary Readings: Isaiah 9:2-7; 62:6-12; 52:7-10; Psalm 96; 97; 98; Titus 2:11-14; 3:4-7; Hebrews 1:1-4 (5-12); Luke 2:1-14 (15-20);John 1:1-14

1st Sunday of Christmas   26

Lectionary Readings: Isaiah 61:10-62:3; Psalm 148; Galatians 4:4-7; Luke 2:22-40

2nd Sunday of Christmas   28

Lectionary Readings: Jeremiah 31:7-14; Psalm 147:12-20; Ephesians 1:3-14; John 1: [1-9] 10-18

Baptism Of Our Lord   30

Lectionary Readings: Genesis 1:1-5; Psalm 29; Acts 19:1-7; Mark 1:4-11

Epiphany 2 — 32

Lectionary Readings: 1 Samuel 3:1-10 (11-20);
Psalm 139:1-6, 13-18; 1 Corinthians 6:12-20; John 1:43-51

Epiphany 3 — 34

Lectionary Readings: Jonah 3:1-5, 10; Psalm 62:5-12;
1 Corinthians 7:29-31; Mark 1:14-20

Epiphany 4 — 36

Lectionary Readings: Deuteronomy 18:15-20; Psalm 111;
1 Corinthians 8:1-13; Mark 1:21-28

Epiphany 5 — 38

Lectionary Readings: Isaiah 40:21-31; Psalm 147: 1-11, 20c;
1 Corinthians 9:16-23; Mark 1:29-39

Epiphany 6 — 40

Lectionary Readings: 2 Kings 5:1-14; Psalm 30;
1 Corinthians 9:24-27; Mark 1:40-45

Transfiguration of Our Lord — 42

Lectionary Readings: 2 Kings 2:1-12; Psalm 50:1-6;
2 Corinthians 4:3-6; Mark 9:2-9

1st Sunday in Lent — 45

Lectionary Readings: Genesis 9:8-17; Psalm 25:1-10; 1 Peter 3:18-22;
Mark 1:9-15

2nd Sunday in Lent — 48

Lectionary Readings: Genesis 17:1-7, 15-16; Psalm 22:23-31;
Romans 4:13-25; Mark 8:31-38

3rd Sunday in Lent   50

Lectionary Readings: Exodus 20:1-17; Psalm 19;
1 Corinthians 1:18-25; John 2:13-22

4th Sunday in Lent   52

Lectionary Readings: Numbers 21:4-9; Psalm 107:1-3, 17-22;
Ephesians 2:1-10; John 3:14-21

5th Sunday in Lent   54

Lectionary Readings: Jeremiah 31:31-34; Psalm 51:1-12; Hebrews 5:5-10;
John 12:20-33

Palm/Passion Sunday   57

Lectionary Readings: Isaiah 50:4-9a; Psalm 31:9-16; Philippians 2:5-11;
Mark 14:1-15:47 or 15:1-39

Maundy Thursday   59

Lectionary Readings: Exodus 12:1-4 (5-10) 11-14; Psalm 116:1-2, 12-19;
1 Corinthians 11:23-26; John 13:1-17, 31b-35

Good Friday   61

Lectionary Readings: Isaiah 52:13-53:12; Psalm 22; Hebrews 10:16-25 or
Hebrews 4:14-16; 5:7-9; John 18:1-19:42

Easter Day   63

Readings: Isaiah 25:6-9 or Acts 10:34-43; Psalm 118:1-2, 14-24;
1 Corinthians 15:1-11; Mark 16:1-8 or John 20:1-18

2nd Sunday of Easter   66

Lectionary Readings: Acts 4:32-35; Psalm 133; 1 John 1:1-2:2;
John 20:19-31

3rd Sunday of Easter 68

Lectionary Readings: Acts 3:12-19; Psalm 4; 1 John 3:1-7; Luke 24:36b-48

4th Sunday of Easter 70

Lectionary Readings: Acts 4:5-12; Psalm 23; 1 John 3:16-24; John 10:11-18

5th Sunday of Easter 72

Lectionary Readings: Acts 8:26-40; Psalm 22:25-31; 1 John 4:7-21; John 15:1-8

6th Sunday of Easter 74

Lectionary Readings: Acts 10:44-48; Psalm 98; 1 John 5:1-6; John 15:9-17

7th Sunday of Easter 76

Lectionary Readings: Acts 1:15-17, 21-26; Psalm 1; 1 John 5:9-13; John 17:6-19

Pentecost Sunday 78

Lectionary Readings: Acts 2:1-21 or Ezekiel 37:1-14; Psalm 104:24-34, 35b; Romans 8:22-27 or Acts 2:1-21; John 15:26-27, 16:4b-15

The Holy Trinity Sunday 81

Lectionary Readings: Isaiah 6:1-8; Psalm 29; Romans 8:12-17; John 3:1-17

Pentecost 2 84

Lectionary Readings: 1 Samuel 8:4-11, (12-15), 16-20, (11:14-15); Psalm 138; 2 Corinthians 4:13-5:1; Mark 3:20-35

Pentecost 3 86

Lectionary Readings: 1 Samuel 15:34-16:13; Psalm 20; 2 Corinthians 5:6-10, (11-13), 14-17; Mark 4:26-34

Pentecost 4   88

Lectionary Readings: 1 Samuel 17:(1a, 4-11, 19-23) 32-49 or
1 Samuel 17:57-18:5, 10-16; Psalm 9:9-20 or Psalm 133;
2 Corinthians 6:1-13; Mark 4:35-41

Pentecost 5   90

Lectionary Readings: 2 Samuel 1:1, 17-27; Psalm 130;
2 Corinthians 8:7-15; Mark 5:21-43

Pentecost 6   92

Lectionary Readings: 2 Samuel 5:1-5, 9-10; Psalm 48;
2 Corinthians 12:2-10; Mark 6:1-13

Pentecost 7   94

Lectionary Readings: Amos 7:7-15; Psalm 85:8-13; Ephesians 1:3-14;
Mark 6:14-29

Pentecost 8   97

Lectionary Readings: 2 Samuel 7:1-14a; Psalm 89:20-37;
Ephesians 2:11-22; Mark 6:30-34, 53-56

Pentecost 9   99

Lectionary Readings: 2 Samuel 11:1-15; Psalm 14; Ephesians 3:14-21;
John 6:1-21

Pentecost 10   101

Lectionary Readings: 2 Samuel 11:26-12:13a; Psalm 51:1-12;
Ephesians 4:1-16; John 6:24-35

Pentecost 11   104

Lectionary Readings: 2 Samuel 18:5-9, 15, 31-33; Psalm 130;
Ephesians 4:25-5:2; John 6:35, 41-51

Pentecost 12   106

Lectionary Readings: 1 Kings 2:10-12; 3:3-14; Psalm 111; Ephesians 5:15-20; John 6:51-58

Pentecost 13   108

Lectionary Readings: 1 Kings 8:(1, 6, 10-11) 22-30, 41-43; Psalm 84; Ephesians 6:10-20; John 6:56-69

Pentecost 14   110

Lectionary Readings: Song of Solomon 2:8-13; Psalm 45:1-2, 6-9; James 1:17-27; Mark 7:1-8, 14-15, 21-23

Pentecost 15   113

Lectionary Readings: Proverbs 22:1-2, 8-9, 22-23; Psalm 125; James 2:1-10 (11-13) 14-17; Mark 7:24-37

Pentecost 16   115

Lectionary Readings: Proverbs 1:20-33; Psalm 19; James 3:1-12; Mark 8:27-38

Pentecost 17   118

Lectionary Readings: Proverbs 31:10-31; Psalm 1; James 3:13-4:3, 7-8a; Mark 9:30-37

Pentecost 18   120

Lectionary Readings: Esther 7:1-6, 9-10; 9:20-22; Psalm 124; James 5:13-20; Mark 9:38-50

Pentecost 19   122

Lectionary Readings: Job 1:1; 2:1-10; Psalm 26; Hebrews 1:1-4; 2:5-12; Mark 10:2-16

Pentecost 20   125

Lectionary Readings: Job 23:1-9, 16-17; Psalm 22:1-15; Hebrews 4:12-16; Mark 10:17-31

Pentecost 21   128

Lectionary Readings: Job 38:1-7 (38-41); Psalm 104:1-9, 24, 35b; Hebrews 5:1-10; Mark 10:35-45

Pentecost 22   130

Lectionary Readings: Job 42:1-6, 10-17; Psalm 34:1-8, (19-22); Hebrews 7:23-28; Mark 10:46-52

Reformation Sunday   132

Lectionary Readings: Jeremiah 31:31-34; Psalm 46; Romans 3:19-28; John 8:31-36

All Saints' Sunday   134

Lectionary Readings: Isaiah 25:6-9 or Wisdom of Solomon 3:1-9; Psalm 24; Revelation 21:1-6a; John 11:32-44

Pentecost 23   137

Lectionary Readings: Ruth 1:1-18; Psalm 146; Hebrews 9:11-14; Mark 12:28-34

Pentecost 24   140

Lectionary Readings: Ruth 3:1-5; 4:13-17; Psalm 127; Hebrews 9:24-28; Mark 12:38-44

Pentecost 25   142

Lectionary Readings: 1 Samuel 1:4-20; 1 Samuel 2:1-10; Psalm 16; Hebrews 10:11-14 (15-18) 19-25; Mark 13:1-8

Christ the King Sunday 145

Lectionary Readings: 2 Samuel 23:1-7; Psalm 132:1-12 [13-18]; Revelations 1:4b-8; John 18:33-37

Thanksgiving Sunday 147

Lectionary Readings: Joel 2:21-27; Psalm 126; 1 Timothy 2:1-7; Matthew 6:25-33

Advent 1

Readings: Isaiah 64:1-9; Psalm 80:1-7, 17-19; 1 Corinthians 1:3-9; Mark 13:24-37

P: God our Father, potter, and redeemer: We stand at the crossroads of a new church year, and commend our lives to you. For the past, present, and future are in your hands; thus we humbly bow before you in awe, wonder, and thanksgiving. God of new beginnings:
C: *Hear our prayer.*

P: God of new life: As we continue our journey into a new year, may we become more open to your marvelous grace. Help us to confess and repent of all wrongdoings; all of our selfish and negative thoughts, words and actions. Aid us taking our anger, grudges, and hurts to you, truly seeking to be reconciled with you and our neighbors. In your sight, all our righteous acts are like filthy rags. Grant us your lovingkindness and forgiveness; mold and fashion us that we may be a more forgiving, loving, caring people. God of new beginnings:
C: *Hear our prayer.*

P: Merciful Lord: In deep gratitude we acknowledge the endless treasures of your grace and peace. As members of the one body of Christ, we lack nothing. Assist us in sharing our God-given gifts with everyone in order that we might all equally participate in the building up of the one body of Christ. God of new beginnings:
C: *Hear our prayer.*

Praying the Lectionary

P: Jesus our Messiah: You teach us that the future is a mystery known only to God the Creator; yet you also want us to be attentive and prepared for the unexpected consummation of your realm. May we walk into the future with hope, trust, confidence, and joy; knowing that one day we shall see you face to face and live with you always. God of new beginnings:
C: *Hear our prayer.*

(Additional intercessions and thanksgivings may be offered here, ending with: God of new beginnings:
C: *Hear our prayer.*)

P: Jesus, our great physician: Today we pray for those among us who are ill in body, mind or soul; especially those whom we name before you now, either aloud or in the silence of our hearts: (NAMES.) God of new beginnings:
C: *Hear our prayer.*

P: Ruler of all nations: Bestow your wisdom and grace upon all political leaders in every land; including Elizabeth our Queen, our Prime Minister and Members of Parliament, our Premier, and Members of the Legislative Assembly, (or other appropriate government leaders and titles for other nations may be added here). May they always protect and serve their most vulnerable citizens and uphold peace with justice, democracy, and freedom for all. God of new beginnings:
C: *Hear our prayer.*

Praying the Lectionary

P: Ever-present God: As we make our pilgrimage into a new church year, broaden our perception to know and experience your multifaceted comings into our world, community and personal lives; that we too may welcome you, saying: "Amen. Come, Lord Jesus! In your name we pray"
ALL: *Amen.*

Advent 2

Readings: Isaiah 40:1-11; Psalm 85:1-2, 8-13; 2; Peter 3:8-15a; Mark 1:1-8

P: Shepherd God: You comfort, restore, and gather all sheep who were scattered to the farthest regions of the earth. Our security rests upon your eternal word, for without it we wither and die like grass. We are thankful for the ancient prophetic vision of restoration, hope, and peace, which speaks to our situation well. You amaze us by revealing your presence in the least expected times and places. Advent God:
C: *We wait and long for your coming.*

P: God of sound and silence: Your tender voice and gentle guidance is beyond comparison and more than what we deserve. We are a sinful people; we desire forgiveness without true repentance; one moment we honor you, the next moment we deny and betray you; we are weak and flighty creatures. O God, have mercy and forgive us! Advent God:
C: *We wait and long for your coming.*

P: God of our journeys: As we travel in the wilderness of this world, our lives seem as if we are on the verge of collapse. Help us to live holy and godly lives; looking to that day when we shall see a new heaven and a new earth. Advent God:
C: *We wait and long for your coming.*

Praying the Lectionary

P: Faithful God: We thank you for the witness of John the Baptizer, who did not seek power and glory for himself; but rather prepared the way for the Messiah with dogged faith and humility. Teach us to be as faithful and humble as John in our discipleship that we may give you the glory and honor, O Christ. Advent God:
C: *We wait and long for your coming.*

(Additional prayers may be included here, ending with: Advent God: **C:** *We wait and long for your coming.*)

P: Lord of every land: We remember the leaders and peoples of every church and state, especially NAMES. Reign over them all so that peace, mercy and justice may be embraced, not only in thoughts and words, but also in actions. Advent God:
C: *We wait and long for your coming.*

P: Jesus our healer: We lift before you all among us who are ill in body, mind or spirit; as well as the dying and those who are mourning their loved ones; whom we name either out loud or in the silence of our hearts before you now: (NAMES.) Advent God:
C: *We wait and long for your coming.*

P: Come Messiah Jesus, to rule our hearts, minds, and lives.
ALL: *Amen.*

Advent 3

Readings: Isaiah 61:1-4, 8-11; Psalm 126 or Luke 1:47-55; 1 Thessalonians 5:16-24; John 1:6-8, 19-28

P: God our liberator: Your power, splendor, and righteousness are extolled by the heavens and the earth. We, in fellowship with the endless throng, praise and adore you. Ever-present God:
C: *In joy we wait for your coming.*

P: Compassionate Lord: The poor, the broken-hearted, the captives, the prisoners, all who mourn are all honored as your precious people. As people who have the luxury of rights, freedoms, and privileges that are denied to almost two-thirds of this world's population; help us to be advocates and ambassadors for the poor, the downtrodden, the hungry, naked, homeless, weak, sick, imprisoned, and dying peoples in our world today. Ever-present God:
C: *In joy we wait for your coming.*

P: Giver of joy: We are indeed grateful for the joy and hope that is ours through your Spirit. We journey into the future with many wonderful aspirations, trusting that our Savior, at the appointed time, shall bestow every good and perfect gift. Ever-present God:
C: *In joy we wait for your coming.*

P: Christ our coming Savior: In our fast-paced lives, we often fail to keep the channels of communication with you open. Forgive us, and help us to be more regular and dis-

Praying the Lectionary

ciplined people of prayer. Ever-present God:
C: *In joy we wait for your coming.*

(Other intercessions and thanksgivings may be added here, ending with: Ever-present God: **C:** *In joy we wait for your coming.*)

P: God of all nations: Guide and inspire all Christians with the power of your Spirit, to live and work for justice and peace in their relations with all people. End all wars and hatreds among the nations of the world. Today we pray especially for the governments and churches of (NAMES.) Ever-present God:
C: *In joy we wait for your coming.*

P: Jesus our great physician: We pray for all among us who are ill in body, mind or soul, as well as for those who are dying and those mourning their loved ones, whom we name now either out loud or in the silence of our hearts: (PAUSE.) Ever-present God:
C: *In joy we wait for your coming.*

P: As John was your humble servant, eager to confess Christ, so may we learn from John's example by lives of humble service and confession; that others may be welcomed into your church.
ALL: *Amen. Come, O true light, and shine in our darkness!*

Advent 4

Readings: 2 Samuel 7:1-11, 16; Psalm 89:1-4, 19-26 or Luke 1:46b-55; Romans 16:25-27; Luke 1:26-38

P: Eternal and holy God: So awesome is your power and presence that heaven and earth are unable to confine you. How all-encompassing is your grace! How magnificent is your reign! God of mercy:
C: *Hear our prayer.*

P: Eternal and holy God: You established a covenant with Israel and the house of David, which opened the way for the coming of the Messiah and the perfection of an everlasting kingdom. We praise and thank you for fulfilling the covenant. God of mercy:
C: Hear our prayer.

P: Eternal and holy God: We thank you for revealing the mystery of eternity to your prophets and apostles, who were empowered by the Holy Spirit to speak and write what had lay hidden for centuries. Help us to cherish this life-giving heritage and share it with others, that all nations might believe and obey you. God of mercy:
C: *Hear our prayer.*

P: Eternal and holy God: As we ponder your workings in the lives of ordinary folk like Mary and Joseph, we are utterly astonished. When you call us to carry out a special task, grant us the enthusiasm, courage, and faith of Mary and Joseph. Equip us with your counselor, that we may

never underestimate your fantastic workings in our lives. God of mercy:
C: *Hear our prayer.*

(Additional prayers may be offered here, ending with: God of mercy: **C:** *Hear our prayer.*)

P: Eternal and holy God: Today we pray for all who are ill among us in body, mind, or soul; and the lonely and depressed, the widows, widowers, and orphans, the unemployed and underemployed, the homeless, hungry and naked; the dying and those who are mourning loved ones, especially those whom we name either aloud or in the silence of our hearts before you now: (PAUSE.) God of mercy:
C: *Hear our prayer.*

P: Eternal and holy God: As our Advent expectation and anticipation move ahead to the Christmas season, we are mindful of the harsh, cold realities of sin and evil in our world today. Come, Jesus our Messiah and establish your perfect reign of love and peace in the hearts, minds and lives of every human being! In your holy name we pray.
ALL: *Amen.*

Christmas Eve or Christmas Day

Readings: Isaiah 9:2-7; 62:6-12; 52:7-10; Psalm 96; 97; 98; Titus 2:11-14; 3:4-7; Hebrews 1:1-4 (5-12); Luke 2:1-14 (15-20); John 1:1-14

P: Holy One of Israel and all nations: On this marvelous festival day, the whole cosmos is united in an unending medley of hymns, prayers, praise, and thanksgivings. All creation bows in adoration and worships you, O blessed holy Trinity! Our lives are overflowing with oceanic joy as we celebrate the birth of Jesus our Messiah! Joy to the world:
C: *The Lord is come!*

P: God of good news: We thank you for your glad tidings as your Holy Spirit winged its way from ancient Israel to the ends of the earth. Bless all who preach, teach, and hear your word; that with the work of your Spirit, all people might see the salvation of our God. Joy to the world:
C: *The Lord is come!*

P: Divine ruler: We are truly grateful that, at the appointed time, the fullness of your majesty and mystery was perfectly revealed in your Son. O Christ, your realm is eternal; we, together with the angels, are subjects of your benevolent reign. Rule over us always, Christ King of kings and Lord of Lords! Joy to the world:
C: *The Lord is come!*

Praying the Lectionary

P: Eternal Word: On this holy day, we celebrate you becoming flesh and dwelling among us. Shine your light into all the darkness of this world — especially where there is oppression, persecution, war, and destruction. May the light you give us reflect outward into the dark places of this world. Joy to the world:
C: *The Lord is come!*

(Additional intercessions and thanksgivings may be included here, ending with: Joy to the world: **C:** *The Lord is come!*)

P: Jesus our healer: Remember on this holy, joyous day, all people who are suffering from loneliness, depression, abuse, poverty, hunger, illnesses, and injustice of all kinds — be they mental, physical, or spiritual. Grant comfort and healing to them all, that they may receive the fullness of your grace and truth. Joy to the world:
C: *The Lord is come!*

P: Grant peace on earth and good will toward all human beings; for the sake of Jesus Christ, the prince of peace. Lead us in the ways of peace, now and always, Jesus our Prince of Peace, in whose holy name we pray.
ALL: *Amen! Hallelujah!*

1st Sunday of Christmas

Readings: Isaiah 61:10-62:3; Psalm 148; Galatians 4:4-7; Luke 2:22-40

P: Lord God our deliverer: We bow before you, as you will cause righteousness and praise to spring up within all the nations. As we continue to celebrate the season of Christmas, we rejoice in the birth of our Messiah who is a crown of beauty in the hand of the Lord, and a royal diadem in God's hand. God of love:
C: *Hear our prayer.*

P: Creator and king: The heavens tell of your glory and praise you, for you commanded and they were created. You established them forever and ever, fixing their bounds. All creatures of earth, sky, and sea tell of your glory and praise you, as do all of the seasons and elements. The human race praises your holy name, for you have raised up a horn for your people. God of love:
C: *Hear our prayer.*

P: God of time and eternity: When the fullness of time had come, you sent your Son Jesus, born under the law, in order to redeem those who were under the law, so that we might be adopted as your children and heirs; for which we are filled with gratitude. God of love:
C: *Hear our prayer.*

P: God of Christmas: Thank you for the examples of Simeon and Anna, who in great patience and devotion to you,

Praying the Lectionary

worshipped and praised the Christ-child. Grant us the patience and devotion of Simeon and Anna, that we too might worship, praise and serve you, Christ, not only this time of the year, but every day. God of love:
C: *Hear our prayer.*

(Other prayers may be added here, ending with: God of love: **C:** *Hear our prayer.*)

P: Christ our great physician: We remember all who are suffering for every manner of sickness and disease — whether of body, mind, or soul, whom we name now either aloud or in the silence of our hearts: (PAUSE.) God of love:
C: *Hear our prayer.*

P: King of kings and Lord of Lords: Rule in the hearts, minds and lives of every leader of every government of every country; that peace with justice, love with mercy would prevail. God of love:
C: *Hear our prayer.*

P: Finally, as we humbly worship the Christ-child in a manger; bestow on us all the means of grace to share his peace with the people of every race, nation, color and creed. In His holy name, we pray.
ALL: *Amen.*

2nd Sunday of Christmas

Readings: Jeremiah 31:7-14; Psalm 147:12-20; Ephesians 1:3-14; John 1: [1-9] 10-18

P: God our loving shepherd: Our hearts and lives delight in you, for you are the true source of joy. We praise and thank you for the gift of joy, as you gather your scattered people from every corner of the Earth to exchange sadness and mourning for joy and gladness. God of grace:
C: *Hear our prayer.*

P: God of all creation: We praise and thank you for your abundance and provision through all the seasons of life. Every season has its beauty and purpose, yielding a multitude of blessings. God of grace:
C: *Hear our prayer.*

P: God our Father: We thank you that, at the appointed time, you adopted us as your children through your Son, Jesus Christ. Thank you for choosing us as your special people; help us through the inspiration of your Spirit, to feed upon your word and that we may always be growing and maturing as Christians. God of grace:
C: *Hear our prayer.*

P: Jesus the word and one true light: We shall never be worthy to express the priceless majesty of your love for us. Help us to live in the fullness of your light, that the darkness of this world may never defeat us. God of grace:
C: *Hear our prayer.*

Praying the Lectionary

P: God of all nations: Our world is burdened with a legion of problems. So often human beings are made to feel as if their lives do not matter, their hearts grow cold in despair, cynicism and apathy. Grant healing and help to the leaders and peoples of every nation. God of grace:
C: *Hear our prayer.*

(Other intercessions and thanksgivings may be offered here, ending with: God of grace: **C:** *Hear our prayer.*)

P: Jesus our healer: There remain many who are in dire need of your healing, today we remember: the sick and dying, those who are mourning loved ones, orphans, widows and widowers, the lonely and depressed, the homeless and naked, the unemployed and underemployed, the refugees, and the ones who are persecuted in your name, and those whom we name now either aloud or in the silence of our hearts: (PAUSE.) God of grace:
C: *Hear our prayer.*

P: Gracious God: As we depart from this place, fill us with your grace and truth, that we may share the true message of Christmas in thought, word, and action by serving you and our neighbors this week. In Jesus' name we pray.
ALL: *Amen.*

Baptism Of Our Lord

Readings: Genesis 1:1-5; Psalm 29; Acts 19:1-7; Mark 1:4-11

P: Maker of heaven and earth: At the dawn of creation your windy, breath-filled Spirit hovered over the chaotic waters, shining light into the darkness and giving life instead to the formless void. In awe and wonder we worship you, God of all creation. God of mercy:
C: *Hear our prayer.*

P: Divine sovereign: You sit enthroned as king forever. Your all-powerful voice spoke the whole universe into existence; everyone and everything ascribes to your glory and strength, and worships you in holy splendor. Open our ears, and our whole being to listen for your voice and be faithful to your ways. May you continue to give strength to your people and bless them with peace. God of mercy:
C: *Hear our prayer.*

P: God of the prophets and apostles: In ancient times, you called John to administer a baptism of repentance for the forgiveness of sins and prepare them for Jesus the Messiah. You also called apostles like Paul to preach your word, baptize in the name of the Lord Jesus, and establish churches throughout the Mediterranean world. As your baptized people, grant us a continuous hunger and thirst for listening to, studying, and practicing your prophetic and apostolic word. God of mercy:

Praying the Lectionary

C: *Hear our prayer.*

P: Jesus, God's beloved Son: We thank you for the sacrament of Holy Baptism, which you have instituted as a gift to your church. Help us to honor our baptism through/with a life of daily repentance and forgiveness and by living the new-resurrected life given through your Holy Spirit. God of mercy:
C: *Hear our prayer.*

(Other thanksgivings and intercessions may be offered here, ending with: God of mercy: **C:** *Hear our prayer.*)

P: Jesus our healer: We remember today all who suffer from various illnesses of the body, mind, and soul; the poor and homeless, the hungry and naked; the refugees; widows, widowers, and orphans; the unemployed and underemployed; the persecuted, tortured, and imprisoned; the victims of abuse of every kind; and all whom we name either out loud or in the silence of our hearts before you now: (PAUSE.) God of mercy:
C: *Hear our prayer.*

P: God of Israel and all nations: Entrust your Spirit of justice and peace to the leaders and citizens of every nation. Increase in everyone the gift of faith, that you may truly be Lord of all. We ask all these prayers and whatever else is in accord with your holy will and purposes, in the name of our Father, Jesus our crucified and risen Messiah, who lives and reigns with you and the Eternal Spirit; one God, forever and ever.
ALL: *Amen.*

Epiphany 2

Readings: 1 Samuel 3:1-10 (11-20); Psalm 139:1-6, 13-18; 1 Corinthians 6:12-20; John 1:43-51

P: God who calls: In ancient times you called people like Eli and Samuel to serve you; and you spoke to them, revealing your holy will. So too today, we are grateful that you call and reveal your will to people of every background imaginable, both young and old, by speaking to us through your word. God of grace:
C: *Hear our prayer.*

P: God who calls: We thank you for the witness of Samuel. Grant us the zeal, sensitivity and openness to you that you gave to him, that we too may listen and obey when you speak to us. God of grace:
C: *Hear our prayer.*

P: God who calls: You have made our bodies the temple of the Holy Spirit. However, we are in a very permissive society, which is opposed to the ethical, moral Christian way of life. By the power and presence of your Spirit in us, help us to be countercultural in our beliefs, values and practices by living God-pleasing lives. God of grace:
C: *Hear our prayer.*

P: God who calls: We thank you for disciples such as Philip and Nathanael; they shared the gospel message with others and invited them to come and see, to accept Jesus as their Messiah. Grant us growth in our faith and disciple-

Praying the Lectionary

ship, that we may become more intentional in our mission and evangelism. God of grace:
C: *Hear our prayer.*
(Additional prayers may be included here, ending with: God of grace: **C:** *Hear our prayer.*)

P: God who calls: Bestow the endless riches of your grace upon the whole Christian church on earth, that your love and truth might increasingly be incarnate in an often cruel and hostile world. Direct and guide all Christians to do their part in the work of justice and peace for a better world. God of grace:
C: *Hear our prayer.*

P: God who calls: We turn to you for healing of body, mind and soul; especially today we remember: (NAMES.) God of grace:
C: *Hear our prayer.*

P: We commend these and all other concerns and requests that may be proper to you, Jesus our Messiah; as we thank, honor, and serve you, who together with the Father and the Holy Spirit remain, one God; now and forever.
ALL: *Amen.*

Epiphany 3

Readings: Jonah 3:1-5, 10; Psalm 62:5-12;
1 Corinthians 7:29-31; Mark 1:14-20

P: Most holy God: You abhor sin and evil; however your compassion toward the truly repentant sinner is boundless in the extreme. We praise and thank you for your never-ending compassion. God of mercy:
C: *Hear our prayer.*

P: God of Israel and the church: We are grateful for providing your people with prophets like Jonah, who proclaimed your word with conviction and led your people to repentance. Help us to heed those who proclaim your word today, that we also may truly repent of our sin like the people of Nineveh. God of mercy:
C: *Hear our prayer.*

P: God of time and eternity: As we live in this world, remind us that human life is but a fleeting moment; we are merely temporary pilgrims here on earth. Remove all of our false securities; that we may not become engrossed in the trappings of this world, but rather live as citizens of your eternal realm. God of mercy:
C: *Hear our prayer.*

P: God of the apostles: We thank you for the examples of discipleship and faith demonstrated by Simon, Andrew, James, and John. You accomplish your incredible deeds even through the most humble and ordinary human be-

ings. May we realize the urgency of your message, O Christ, and swiftly answer your call to discipleship and faith. God of mercy:
C: *Hear our prayer.*

(Additional intercessions and thanksgivings may be offered here, ending with: God of mercy: **C:** *Hear our prayer.*)

P: Lord of all nations: May the path of your Spirit's sway grow to include the governments and people of this and every land, that the quality of life may be enhanced and enriched for the whole human race and all of creation. God of mercy:
C: *Hear our prayer.*

P: Jesus our healer: We remember today all among us who are ill in body, mind and soul, as well as those who are dying or are mourning loved ones: (NAMES). Grant them your healing presence, peace, and comfort. God of mercy:
C: *Hear our prayer.*

P: Hear our prayers O triune God, even as we pray:
ALL: *Our Father…*

Epiphany 4

Readings: Deuteronomy 18:15-20; Psalm 111; 1 Corinthians 8:1-13; Mark 1:21-28

P: Eternal God: Your divine greatness is shrouded in majesty and mystery, but your compassionate nearness is incarnate in Jesus Christ. We celebrate your presence among us and bow in adoration and reverence of you, O blessed one. God of the church:
C: *Make us one in Christ, and hear our prayer.*

P: God of the prophets: We thank you for the noble legacy of your prophets, especially in the person of Jesus. Today there are many false prophets who, on the surface, attract, entertain, and offer extremely easy answers to many of life's complex questions. Protect us and all people from falling prey to such charlatans, who disguise themselves as true prophets. God of the church:
C: *Make us one in Christ, and hear our prayer.*

P: Gracious Lord: We rejoice in being the recipients of your true knowledge and love, accompanied by a fantastic freedom. Bestow your Spirit upon us, that we may administer this knowledge, love, and freedom you have given us with all others, through your wisdom, gentleness, humility, and great care; through this, our weaker sisters and brothers may become stronger and more mature in their Christian faith. God of the church:
C: *Make us one in Christ, and hear our prayer.*

Praying the Lectionary

P: Jesus our greatest teacher and healer: The human race continues to marvel at your teaching authority and yearn for your healing power and presence. Help all members of your church to believe and obey your teachings, to share your healing power and presence with those who are deeply troubled in mind, body or spirit. Today especially we remember: (NAMES.) God of the church:
C: *Make us one in Christ, and hear our prayer.*

(Special intercessions and thanksgivings may be offered here, ending with: God of the church: **C:** *Make us one in Christ, and hear our prayer.*)

P: Lord of the church: We pray for the work and ministry of all the Christian churches around the world; bless and prosper them as they serve you and your holy purposes. God of the church:
C: *Make us one in Christ, and hear our prayer.*

P: Grant peace, mercy, and justice to all leaders and peoples on Earth; we pray in the name of Jesus our Savior, teacher and healer.
ALL: *Amen.*

Epiphany 5

Readings: Isaiah 40:21-31; Psalm 147: 1-11, 20c; 1 Corinthians 9:16-23; Mark 1:29-39

P: Holy one of heaven and earth: Who is able to fathom the vast treasures of your grace? The whole universe is filled with awe and wonder. You do not faint or grow weary; your understanding is unsearchable. You give power to the faint and strengthen the powerless. Those who wait for you, Lord, shall renew their strength; they shall mount up with wings like eagles, they shall run and not become weary, they shall walk and not become faint. God of mercy:
C: *Hear our prayer.*

P: Gracious God: We praise you. You heal the brokenhearted and bind up their wounds. You lift up the downtrodden, and cast the wicked to the ground. You give hope to those who fear you, that they might receive your steadfast love. Today we turn to you for those among us who are in need of healing in body, mind, or soul; we name them before you now either out loud or in the silence of our hearts: (PAUSE.) God of mercy:
C: *Hear our prayer.*

P: Jesus our Messiah: We thank you for Paul the apostle and all other servants of your gospel who have made great personal sacrifices, in order that many people might become members of the church. Grant your Spirit's blessings upon all servants of your gospel today, that all who hear

Praying the Lectionary

your preached word may believe and follow you. God of mercy:
C: *Hear our prayer.*

P: Jesus our Savior: in your earthly ministry, you stressed the nearness of God's realm by preaching the good news with authority and healing illnesses of every description. In a world beset by hatred, destruction and countless illnesses, defend and prosper the church's ministry of preaching the good news and healing people of every nation. God of mercy:
C: *Hear our prayer.*

(Additional prayers may be included here, ending with: God of mercy: **C:** *Hear our prayer.*)

P: Lord of all nations: Look with favor upon the governments and citizens and churches of every land; all that serve those who are in greatest need in your name are also administering justice and peace amongst your people. God of mercy:
C: *Hear our prayer.*

P: As we go our separate ways this week, grant us forgiveness and healing, that we too may strive to forgive and be a healing, caring presence in our relationships with others. In the name of Jesus, the light of the world, we pray.
ALL: *Amen.*

Epiphany 6

Lectionary Readings: 2 Kings 5:1-14; Psalm 30; 1 Corinthians 9:24-27; Mark 1:40-45

P: God our Creator and healer: You govern the sick and healthy, the dying and living. We give you our praise and thanks for the priceless gift of life and healing. God of life:
C: *Have mercy on us.*

P: God our Creator and healer: We thank you for the healing ministry of your prophet Elisha, who cured Naaman of his leprosy. We rejoice that, in our baptism you acted mightily to cure us of the age-old disease of sin, which has been conquered through Jesus Christ our Savior. God of life:
C: *Have mercy on us.*

P: God our Creator and healer: We give you thanks for the ministries of Paul and countless other disciples through the ages. Help us to honor their legacy by learning from them and following their example. God of life:
C: *Have mercy on us.*

P: God our Creator and healer: We confess, that on occasion our flippant, undisciplined attitude toward the Christian faith and life has caused ourselves, others, you and your church pain and suffering. Forgive us, discipline us, and help us to run the race and glimpse the winning prize, your kingdom of Heaven. God of life:
C: *Have mercy on us.*

Praying the Lectionary

P: God our Creator and healer: We thank you, Jesus, for your endless compassion, which knows no partiality. Grant us your Holy Spirit, that we may reflect your compassion to others. God of life:
C: *Have mercy on us.*

(Additional thanksgivings and intercessions may be offered here, ending with: God of life: **C:** *Have mercy on us.*)

P: God our Creator and healer: Befriend the lonely, lift the spirits of the depressed, comfort the suffering and grieving, grant food to the hungry, clothing for the naked, shelter for the homeless, work for the unemployed and underemployed, peace for the victims of war and violence. Cleanse and cure all infirmities of body, mind or spirit, whom we name either aloud or in the silence of our hearts before you now: (PAUSE.) God of life:
C: *Have mercy on us.*

P: God our Creator and healer: We pray for Elizabeth our Queen, our Prime Minister and Members of Parliament, our Premier and Members of the Legislative Assembly, (or other appropriate government leaders and titles for other nations may be added here); and the heads of state in every land: Grant them your grace and wisdom to govern responsibly in the service of justice and peace for all peoples. God of life:
C: *Have mercy on us.*

P: We commend these and all other prayers to you, Jesus, our great physician and compassionate Savior, who taught us how to pray:
ALL: *Our Father… Amen.*

Transfiguration of Our Lord

Readings: 2 Kings 2:1-12; Psalm 50:1-6;
2 Corinthians 4:3-6; Mark 9:2-9

P: God of the Israelites and the prophets; God of your Son, Jesus and his apostles; God of the human race — how magnificent is your reign over all creation. Your divine glory is awe-inspiring and your coming to us in the human form of Jesus is enlightening. We praise and thank you, O blessed One. God of Transfiguration:
C: *Have mercy on us.*

P: Ancient of days: We thank you for the faithful witness of Elijah and Elisha. Grant us a generous portion of your Spirit, that we too may be your faithful witnesses. God of Transfiguration:
C: *Have mercy on us.*

P: Covenant-making God: We are indeed grateful that, in Christ, we inherit a new covenant which has removed the veil that blinded us and has given us an enormous freedom. Help us to become more mature and discerning Christians, that we may live by the truth and authenticity of your word. God of Transfiguration:
C: *Have mercy on us.*

P: Transfigured Christ: Our lives at times seem to be filled with noise and clutter; rarely do we set aside adequate time and space to worship you. Forgive us for neglecting you in our daily agendas. God of Transfiguration:

Praying the Lectionary

C: *Have mercy on us.*

P: Christ, light of the world: As we seek to worship you in spirit and truth, grant a clearer vision, embrace us with your presence, and remove our obsessions with the troubles of this world. In the peace and quiet of worship, strengthen and equip us to boldly share your vision and presence with an often chaotic, threatening world. God of Transfiguration:
C: *Have mercy on us.*

(Other prayers may be added here, ending with: God of Transfiguration: **C:** *Have mercy on us.*)

P: Christ our great physician: Today we pray for all among us who are ill in body, mind or soul, who we name before you either aloud or in the silence of our hearts: (PAUSE.) God of Transfiguration:
C: *Have mercy on us.*

P: Ruler of all nations: Bestow your gifts and fruit of the Holy Spirit upon the leaders of every nation, including Elizabeth our Queen, our Prime Minister and Members of Parliament, our Premier and Members of the Legislative Assembly, (or other appropriate government leaders and titles for other nations may be added here) that peace, justice, freedom and democracy may prevail in our land and in every other nation of the world. God of Transfiguration:
C: *Have mercy on us.*

P: As we celebrate your bright radiance, O Transfigured Christ; may your light shine in and through us, this week

and all weeks, so that others may see your glory. In your holy name we pray.
ALL: *Amen.*

1st **Sunday in Lent**

Readings: Genesis 9:8-17; Psalm 25:1-10;
1 Peter 3:18-22; Mark 1:9-15

P: Maker of heaven and earth: We praise and thank you that long ago, you made an everlasting covenant with every living creature of all flesh that is on the earth. You love your creation, and the sign of your covenant of love is the rainbow in the heavens, reminding us that you will never destroy the earth again by flood. God of mercy:
C: *Hear our prayer.*

P: God of steadfast love: We are most grateful that you do not remember the sins of our youth. Rather, you are good and upright, instructing sinners in the your ways, and leading the humble in what is right. God of mercy:
C: *Hear our prayer.*

P: Christ our suffering servant: You suffered for sins, once for all, the righteous for the unrighteous, in order to bring the human race to God. We thank you, that through baptism we are united with your death and resurrection and we are able to worship and serve you as the Holy One at God's right hand with angels, authorities, and powers made subject to you. God of mercy:
C: *Hear our prayer.*

P: Christ our perfect example: As you were thrown out into the wilderness by the Holy Spirit to be tempted and tested by the powers of evil for forty days, you succeed-

ed in resisting all temptations. So may we, during these forty days of Lent, resist the temptations facing us. After resisting all temptations, you set out to preach the gospel with the message of the nearness of God's kingdom and the need to repent and believe the good news. So may we, during these forty days of Lent, hear the preaching of the gospel message, look for the signs of the nearness of God's kingdom, repent of our sins, and believe the good news. God of mercy:
C: *Hear our prayer.*

(Other thanksgivings and intercessions may be included here, ending with: God of mercy: **C:** *Hear our prayer.*)

P: Lord of all nations: We pray for the leaders, peoples, and churches of our nation and every nation, that all people would beat swords into ploughshares; that, as one human family, we would all strive for peace, mercy and justice in the whole world. God of mercy:
C: *Hear our prayer.*

P: Gracious God: During this Lenten season, make us ever mindful of the tremendous sacrifice you made for us, O God; that we, in our own small way, may be inspired and empowered to make sacrifices of our time, talents, money, and whatever else is proper for your sake and the sake of your realm. God of mercy:
C: *Hear our prayer.*

P: Divine healer: today we remember all among us who are ill in body, mind or soul, especially those whom we name before now either out loud, or in the silence of our

Praying the Lectionary

hearts, (PAUSE.) God of mercy:
C: *Hear our prayer.*

P: All of these things and whatever is wholesome and proper, we ask in the name of our blessed Holy Trinity; Father, Son, and Holy Spirit.
ALL: *Amen.*

2nd **Sunday in Lent**

Readings: Genesis 17:1-7, 15-16; Psalm 22:23-31; Romans 4:13-25; Mark 8:31-38

P: Ancient of days: We praise and thank you that through Abraham and Sarah you were able to give new life, new birth and new hope to them in the old age by making an everlasting covenant with them. We praise and thank you too for giving us new life, new birth, new hope by making your covenant with us through your Son Jesus, our Lord and Savior. God of mercy:
C: *Hear our prayer.*

P: Lord God: All the ends of the earth shall remember and turn to you; all the families of the nations shall worship before you. For dominion belongs to you, ruler over the nations. Bestow your wisdom and guidance upon all governments of every land — that they may serve their citizens by upholding and maintaining democracy, freedom, justice, and peace. God of mercy:
C: *Hear our prayer.*

P: Gracious God: We are most grateful that we receive your promises and are justified not by work or the law, but by grace through faith in Jesus, our cross-bearing Savior. We thank you for the example of Abraham and Sarah; their faith was reckoned to them as righteousness as they believed in your promise to them. So may we trust in your promise to us, that through Jesus' death and resurrection

Praying the Lectionary

we are justified, made righteous, and given eternal life. God of mercy:
C: *Hear our prayer.*

P: Christ our cross-bearing Savior: The world constantly tempts us to live a life of ease, full of comfort and selfish pleasures. Grant us the grace to resist these ever-present temptations by a life of self-denial and cross-bearing servanthood. In the face of persecution and growing hostility toward you and your church, empower and strengthen us in our faith and integrity toward you and your gospel. We ask for faith, courage and strength to deny ourselves, take up our crosses, and follow you. God of mercy:
C: *Hear our prayer.*

(Additional prayers may be offered here, ending with: God of mercy: **C:** *Hear our prayer.*)

P: Great physician: We pray for all among us who suffer from illnesses of the mind, body or soul; especially today we remember: (PAUSE.) God of mercy:
C: *Hear our prayer.*

P: In the name of Jesus our cross-bearing servant, Savior and Lord, we offer these prayers to you and commend our lives and all that is ours into your care.
ALL: *Amen.*

3rd Sunday in Lent

Readings: Exodus 20:1-17; Psalm 19;
1 Corinthians 1:18-25; John 2:13-22

P: God of liberation: We are truly grateful for the freedom that comes from you. We are mindful of all the people in our time who continue to suffer in various forms of slavery and oppression. Save all who are the victims of violence, poverty and discrimination from despair and helplessness. Grant freedom to your people who are enslaved and oppressed. God of grace:
C: *Have mercy on us.*

P: Loving Creator: We thank you for your commandments, which are not only guidelines for society as a whole and ourselves personally, but also a sign of your magnificent and endless love toward us. Help us to live by your commandments out of love for you. God of grace:
C: *Have mercy on us.*

P: Christ our suffering servant: As we move ahead on our Lenten journey, grant us the wisdom and strength of the crucified Christ, that we may be effective messengers of your kingdom. May the preaching of Christ crucified open up new possibilities for the Christian church to minister to our troubled and broken world. May we follow you and be more faithful cross-bearers. God of grace:
C: *Have mercy on us.*

Praying the Lectionary

(Additional thanksgivings and intercessions may be included here, ending with: God of grace: **C:** *Have mercy on us.*)

P: Ruler of all nations: We pray for your provision of abundant grace to the peoples and leaders of all nations, that a spirit of peace and justice might wing its way throughout the whole inhabited earth. May the transforming power of your abundant grace take root in us all. God of grace:
C: *Have mercy on us.*

P: Christ our great physician: We remember all among us who are ill in body, mind or spirit, especially those whom we name either out loud or in the silence of our hearts before you now: (PAUSE.) God of grace:
C: *Have mercy on us.*

P: Bless the whole body of Christ on earth; inspire, correct, defend and nurture all Christians. Enable all Christians to worship you in spirit and in truth. We commend all of these our prayers and whatever else may be in accord with your will and purposes, in the name of Christ our cross-bearing Savior.
ALL: *Amen.*

4th Sunday in Lent

Readings: Numbers 21:4-9; Psalm107:1-3, 17-22; Ephesians 2:1-10; John 3:14-21

P: O God, Creator and lover of this world: We praise and thank you for the gift of life. We are often complacent and fail to appreciate the great riches of your grace, mercy and love at work in the world every day. Help us to be less complacent and more grateful for the gift of life you have given us. God of grace:
C: *Have mercy on us.*

P: Saving God: In the grace and freedom of Jesus Christ, we are given opportunities every day to do good works, knowing full well that good works do not save us; rather, they are a faithful and free response to you. Make us all more willing to fill our days in humble service. God of grace:
C: *Have mercy on us.*

P: Compassionate God: The majesty of your love far exceeds our human comprehension. In your love for the entire world, you continue to protect, preserve, and restore all of creation. Grant us hope and determination that, whatever our status, we might resist the powers of evil, deceit, and destruction at work in the world. Make us your instruments of truth, life, and light in the world. God of grace:
C: *Have mercy on us.*

Praying the Lectionary

P: As Jesus Christ was lifted up on the cross to embrace all of creation with God's saving, life-giving power, we ask that the body of Christ in the world today might faithfully bear the cross and thus enable the whole world to believe in you. Help your church to live faithfully in the world. God of grace:
C: *Have mercy on us.*

(Other prayers may be offered here, ending with: God of grace: **C:** *Have mercy on us.*)

P: Christ our healer: Today we pray for all among us who are ill in body, mind, or spirit, whom we name either aloud or in the silence of our hearts before you now: (PAUSE.) God of grace:
C: *Have mercy on us.*

P: Heavenly king: Today we pray for Elizabeth our Queen, our Prime Minister and Members of Parliament, our Premier and Members of the Legislative Assembly, (or other appropriate government leaders and titles for other nations may be added here) as well as the governments of every land. Bestow on them your grace and wisdom, that they may humbly serve you and all of their citizens by upholding justice and peace, freedom, and democracy. God of grace:
C: *Have mercy on us.*

P: In acknowledgement of our eternal interdependence upon you Lord God and your creation, we entrust our prayers and our lives to you in the name of Jesus the Messiah, Savior of the world.
ALL: *Amen.*

5th Sunday in Lent

Readings: Jeremiah 31:31-34; Psalm 51:1-12; Hebrews 5:5-10; John 12:20-33

P: Covenant-making God: Ruler over the old and the new, God of time and eternity; God the covenant-giver; fickle and frail creatures of dust that we are, a lifetime is far too brief to praise and thank you. In awe and adoration, we bow before you. God of mercy:
C: *Hear our prayer.*

P: Covenant-making God: Remove the clutter in our lives, draw us closer to you that we might know you more intimately and live according to your covenant-promise. Open our hearts to live by your grace. God of mercy:
C: *Hear our prayer.*

P: Covenant-making God: In trust and obedience, following the example of Jesus, help us to be more regular and disciplined people of prayer. Rooted in prayer, you teach us the deeper meaning and purpose of life. God of mercy:
C: *Hear our prayer.*

P: Covenant-making God: We are your seeds, O Lord; help us to grow and produce much fruit. Grant us a never-ending hunger and thirst for your gospel, that as we are fed and filled full-to-overflowing, we might share this heavenly food with other hungry and thirsty people. Help us to be your productive seeds. God of mercy:
C: *Hear our prayer.*

Praying the Lectionary

P: Covenant-making God: Our world worships material possessions, comfort and glamour, but you, O Christ, teach that we must die to these things if we are to live a rich and full life. May the movement of your Spirit penetrate the hearts and lives of all people; may the values of your kingdom produce peace, justice and harmony in the whole world. Bless, protect, and guide all peoples, churches, and nations of the world. God of mercy:
C: *Hear our prayer.*

P: Covenant-making God: We pray for the whole Christian church around the globe; break the tyranny of spiritual, self-righteous pride and sin, remove the barriers which divide Christians from one another, protect and defend our sisters and brothers who live under persecution, poverty and injustice. Bestow the means of grace on us all to faithfully do your will. God of mercy:
C: *Hear our prayer.*

(Other intercessions and thanksgivings may be added here, ending with: God of mercy: **C:** *Hear our prayer.*)

P: Covenant-making God: You care for and comfort all who are sick, lonely, depressed, suffering, persecuted, poor, unemployed or underemployed, widowed and orphaned, the dying, and those grieving loved ones. Today we remember such persons among us, and name them either out loud or in the silence of our hearts before you now: (PAUSE.) God of mercy:
C: *Hear our prayer.*

Praying the Lectionary

P: We pray these prayers in the name of our glorified and crucified Lord and Savior Jesus, whose power draws all people to himself.

ALL: *Amen.*

Palm/Passion Sunday

Readings: Isaiah 50:4-9a; Psalm 31:9-16; Philippians 2:5-11; Mark 14:1-15:47 or 15:1-39

P: Holy and almighty God: Today we join the ranks of countless sinner-saints shouting loud hosannas as Jesus makes his triumphant, yet humble entry into Jerusalem. We have come from our homes, schools and workplaces to worship and honor Jesus our Lord and king. Hosanna to Jesus our Lord and king! God of grace:
C: *Have mercy on us.*

P: Jesus our suffering servant: Our celebrating is mingled with grieving as the events of your passion unfold; we, together with the entire human race nailed you to the cross at Golgotha. The betrayal of Judas, the denial of Peter, the scheming of the Jewish leaders, the corruption of the Roman leaders, the rejection of the crowds and the abandonment of the disciples, remind us all that we continue to share the responsibility of similar crimes and sins. Forgive us, Jesus our Lord and king! God of grace:
C: *Have mercy on us.*

P: Cross-bearing Savior: May your Spirit be with us as we embark upon our journey into Holy Week. Lighten our darkness and make us keenly aware of the priceless gift that is ours through your passion and death. We and the whole creation are given a new destiny, thanks to the passion and death of Jesus our Lord and king. God of grace:
C: *Have mercy on us.*

Praying the Lectionary

P: Lord of the nations: Pour out your super-abundant grace, that it may flow into every corner of the world, especially among peoples living in the world's poorest countries and wherever there is famine, persecution and war. Reign over the leaders and peoples of every tribe, race and creed, Jesus our Lord and king. God of grace:
C: *Have mercy on us.*

(Additional prayers may be offered here, ending with: God of grace: **C:** *Have mercy on us.*)

P: Christ our great physician: Today we remember all among us who are suffering from illness and disease of body, mind or soul, especially those whom we name aloud or in the silence of our hearts before you now: (PAUSE.) God of grace:
C: *Have mercy on us.*

P: Lord of the church: The world is beset by changes, turmoil, unrest and other marks of sin and evil. In the midst of all this, grant your whole church vision, courage, understanding, and compassion to faithfully preach and live your gospel kingdom. Bestow upon us your mind, your obedience, your servanthood, Jesus our Lord and king. We pray in the name of Jesus our crucified Lord and king.
ALL: *Amen.*

Maundy Thursday

Readings: Exodus 12:1-4 (5-10) 11-14;
Psalm 116:1-2, 12-19; 1 Corinthians 11:23-26;
John 13:1-17, 31b-35

P: God our deliverer: We praise and thank you for saving your chosen people by commanding them to observe the Passover and place the lamb's blood on their doors. You also save us through Jesus, our Passover Lamb, whose shed blood makes us righteous in your sight and offers us forgiveness of sin. God of mercy:
C: *Hear our prayer.*

P: God our deliverer: As you led the ancient Israelites out of slavery into freedom and a land of promise; deliver and lead all peoples today out of their various forms of slavery into freedom. May we, like the psalmist of old, offer to you a thanksgiving sacrifice and call on your name O Lord, and serve you faithfully all our days. God of mercy:
C: *Hear our prayer.*

P: God our deliverer: We praise and thank you, that on this night when you were betrayed, you instituted the sacrament of Holy Communion. You promised that through the celebration of your Holy Supper, you are present with us and we remember that you have forgiven our sins and established a life-giving covenant with us. God of mercy:
C: *Hear our prayer.*

Praying the Lectionary

P: God our deliverer: On this night, you also set an example for your followers of every age to wash one another's feet as a sign of true, humble service. You also gave your disciples a new commandment to love one another as you have loved us. By this love, everyone will know that we are your disciples. May your Spirit help us to keep this new commandment. God of mercy:
C: *Hear our prayer.*

(Additional intercessions and thanksgivings may be included here, ending with: God of mercy: **C:** *Hear our prayer.*)

P: God our deliverer: Send us your Spirit, heal our brokenness, unite your fragmented body, guide those who are lost, correct those who err, befriend those who are lonely, comfort those who are sick, suffering, or dying, provide for and defend the poor and powerless especially those who we lift before you, silently and aloud (Pause). Make us more willing servants that we might minister more effectively to the needs of others. God of mercy:
C: *Hear our prayer.*

P: O Lamb of God, suffering servant, crucified Lord and king, high priest of all humanity: You have promised to have mercy upon us and hear our prayers. We commend all this into your care and whatever else may be proper and wholesome for us, in the name of our one true God, Father, Son, and Holy Spirit.
ALL: *Amen.*

Good Friday

Readings: Isaiah 52:13-53:12; Psalm 22; Hebrews 10:16-25 or Hebrews 4:14-16; 5:7-9; John 18:1-19:42

P: Loving God: On this holiest of days we, together with all creation, bow in awe and wonder to worship you. We are completely humbled and filled with gratitude when you, on this day, offer us and all humankind the precious gift of life in the person of Jesus Christ crucified. Surely he has borne our griefs and carried our diseases. God of mercy:
C: *Hear our prayer.*

P: Ancient of days: An eternity is far too short to worship and serve you. We will never, ever be able to repay you, Jesus, Savior of the world for what you accomplished on that first Good Friday. For we, along with the whole human race, crucified you, and continue to crucify you. He was despised and rejected by others; all we like sheep have gone astray; and the Lord has laid on him the sin of us all. God of mercy:
C: *Hear our prayer.*

P: Jesus our suffering servant: Today your power and love is poured out on the cross and embraces every corner of the earth. You are the Savior of the poor and oppressed, the handicapped and disabled, the innocent who are victimized by diabolical acts of cruelty and torture, the countless millions who suffer because of their skin color, or their gender, or the country of their birth. We confess that all

Praying the Lectionary

too often we are the beneficiaries of unjust and discriminatory systems: forgive us and help us to live a lifestyle of justice and peace. God of mercy:
C: *Hear our prayer.*

P: Jesus our Master, friend and brother: You have given us the true meaning and purpose of life; namely, that in life there is death and in death there is life. Help your church to live and proclaim this message to the whole world. Rule over our bodies, minds, and spirits that we may accomplish your will and bear the cross you have given each one of us. God of mercy:
C: *Hear our prayer.*

(Other prayers may be offered here, ending with: God of mercy: **C:** *Hear our prayer.*)

P: Have mercy and hear our prayer, most holy God; for the sake of Jesus your son, who suffered and died on the tree at Golgotha for us all.
ALL: *Amen.*

Easter Day

Readings: Isaiah 25:6-9 or Acts 10:34-43; Psalm 118:1-2, 14-24; 1 Corinthians 15:1-11; Mark 16:1-8 or John 20:1-18

P: All-powerful and ever-living God: We celebrate this festival day with joy and thanksgiving. You have won a marvelous victory over the powers of evil, sin and death! Alleluia! We rejoice in the resurrection of Jesus our Lord and Savior! This is the day that the Lord has made:
C: *We shall rejoice and be glad in it!*

(An alternative congregational response may be to sing the refrain of an Easter song, such as "Alleluia, Alleluia, Give Thanks" after each intercession.)

P: All-powerful and ever-living God: This day we join together with everyone in the celebration of your triumphant feast which you have prepared for us. You have wiped away our tears of sadness and filled us with the joy and hope of new life. We are filled-to-overflowing with the splendid riches of your victory feast, O risen Christ! This is the day that the Lord has made:
C: *We shall rejoice and be glad in it!*

P: All-powerful and ever-living God: In your resurrection, time and eternity meet; the human family, along with all of creation have, in a wonderful way, been restored from death back to life. As the firstfruits represent the abundance of the whole harvest, so too Christ's resurrection

Praying the Lectionary

represents the abundant life we will share with him when we are raised from the dead. This is the day that the Lord has made:
C: *We shall rejoice and be glad in it!*

P: All-powerful and ever-living God: On that first Easter morning, you rolled away the stone from the door of the tomb. The women discovered an empty tomb and a risen Jesus. In a similar manner, roll away our stones of fear and doubt, that we too might discover more clearly a risen Jesus living among us today. Shine upon us with the brightness of your resurrected light, O risen one. This is the day that the Lord has made:
C: *We shall rejoice and be glad in it!*

(Other intercessions and thanksgivings may be included here, ending with: This is the day that the Lord has made:
C: *We shall rejoice and be glad in it!*)

P: All-powerful and ever-living God: Today we pray for all among us who are suffering from illnesses of mind, body or soul; whom we name either out loud or in the silence of our hearts before you now: (PAUSE.) This is the day that the Lord has made:
C: *We shall rejoice and be glad in it!*

P: All-powerful and ever-living God: Grant us your Spirit's presence, that we may bask in the sheer delight of your all-sufficient grace now and always. In loving response to this precious grace, help us to freely serve you, one another and the whole creation. Assist us as we share the new life of our risen Master with the whole world. This is the

Praying the Lectionary

day that the Lord has made:
C: *We shall rejoice and be glad in it!*

P: All of this we pray in the name of our risen Savior, Jesus Christ. Alleluia!
ALL: *Amen.*

2nd Sunday of Easter

Readings: Acts 4:32-35; Psalm 133; 1 John 1:1-2:2; John 20:19-31

P: Gracious God: We praise and thank you for filling the first-generation Christians with your grace, that they willingly shared all of their resources with one another so that there was not a needy person among them. In our part of the world, we confess that many are filled with greed, and lack a spirit of generosity toward those in need. Forgive us Lord, for our selfishness and unwillingness to share with those in need what you have so generously given us. God of mercy:
C: *Hear our prayer.*

P: Lord of all: As the psalmist long ago knew so well: How very good and pleasant it is when kindred live together in unity! May the precious oil and dew of Hermon bring healing and unity among us, that we may be blessed with life forevermore. God of mercy:
C: *Hear our prayer.*

P: God of light: In you there is no darkness at all. Bestow on us your Spirit that we may walk in the light; have fellowship with one another, and be cleansed from all sin by the blood of Jesus. As we confess our sins to you and one another, cleanse us, forgive us, and help us to forgive one another. God of mercy:
C: *Hear our prayer.*

Praying the Lectionary

P: Risen Christ: At times, the doubts and fears in our hearts and minds cause us to be skeptical and not to believe. We, like Thomas, would much rather see you first and only then believe in you. Grant us your grace to number us among those who have not seen and yet still believe. Fill us with your peace, in our personal lives, and in the lives of all Christians around the world — that wars might end, prejudice and hatred might be transformed into cooperation and love, and your Holy Spirit might breathe the breath of new life into us and the whole body of Christ. Send us out into the world as your ambassadors of peace. God of mercy:
C: *Hear our prayer.*

(Additional prayers may be offered here, ending with: God of mercy: **C:** *Hear our prayer.*)

P: Christ our healer: Today we remember all among us who are ill in body, mind, or soul, especially those whom we name before you now either out loud or in the silence of our hearts: (PAUSE.) God of mercy:
C: *Hear our prayer.*

P: Hear our prayers, have mercy on us, reign over us, inspire us, enable us to be your faithful disciples, O risen Christ; for we commend our hearts, minds, bodies, souls and all that is ours to you, the one God, who lives and reigns with the Holy Spirit, now and forever.
ALL: *Amen.*

3rd Sunday of Easter

Readings: Acts 3:12-19; Psalm 4; 1 John 3:1-7; Luke 24:36b-48

P: God of our ancestors: We worship you for glorifying your servant Jesus by raising him from the dead. We also are most grateful for the strong witnesses of the resurrection through the apostles. May we too be your witnesses by sharing our faith with others. God of grace:
C: *Hear our prayer.*

P: God of light and life: You hear us when we call to you in times of need, and we place our trust in you. Let the light of your face shine on us, O Lord. Put gladness in our hearts; for you alone make us lie down in safety. God of grace:
C: *Hear our prayer.*

P: Heavenly Father: You have given us your constant love and have called us your children. We thank you that through Jesus our sins are taken away, for in him there is no sin, and he has made us righteous. God of grace:
C: *Hear our prayer.*

P: Risen Christ: As you came to the first disciples and gave them your peace, so too you come today and offer us your peace. After showing yourself to the first disciples and eating, you opened the disciples' minds to understand the scriptures, that they might be your witnesses beginning from Jerusalem to all nations. Thanks to the faithfulness of

Praying the Lectionary

the apostles, faith has been passed on from generation to generation, even to us today. God of grace:
C: *Hear our prayer.*

(Additional intercessions and thanksgivings may be included here, ending with: God of grace: **C:** *Hear our prayer.*)

P: Jesus our great physician: Today we remember those among us who are ill in body, mind, or soul, especially: (NAMES.) God of grace:
C: *Hear our prayer.*

P: Lord of all nations: Grant your wisdom to Elizabeth our Queen, our Prime Minister and Members of Parliament, our Premier and Members of the Legislative Assembly, (or other appropriate government leaders and titles for other nations may be added here), our mayor and council members, and the leaders of all nations; that they may govern with peace and justice and uphold freedom and democracy. God of grace:
C: *Hear our prayer.*

P: Christ, head of the church: We pray for your blessing upon all Christians around the world, that the message of the gospel would reach out to all people. God of grace:
C: *Hear our prayer.*

P: All of these our prayers, and whatever else that may be in accord with your holy will and purposes, we commend to you O Christ, our risen Savior and Lord.
ALL: *Amen.*

4th Sunday of Easter

Readings: Acts 4:5-12; Psalm 23; 1 John 3:16-24; John 10:11-18

P: Lord God: We praise and thank you that in raising Jesus from the dead, we are given a sign of future hope. Jesus is now our cornerstone; there is no other name under heaven given among mortals by which we must be saved. God of mercy:
C: *Hear our prayer.*

P: God our shepherd: You so generously provide for all of our needs. You walk with us even in our most difficult times of life, including death. You are our generous host; giving us both earthly and heavenly food and drink. You pursue us with your goodness and mercy each day of our life; and we look forward to that day when we shall live in your house forever. God of mercy:
C: *Hear our prayer.*

P: God of love: We are filled with gratitude for you have loved us sinners so much that you laid down your life for us. In response to your never-ending love for us, help us to lay down our lives for one another in love, and so abide in your love by sharing our time, talents, and finances with those in need. God of mercy:
C: *Hear our prayer.*

P: Jesus our Good Shepherd: You have laid down your life for us. You know us better than we know ourselves. Open our hearts, minds, ears, and eyes to listen for your voice

Praying the Lectionary

and follow you wherever you lead us we pray; that there may be one flock under you, our one true shepherd. God of mercy:
C: *Hear our prayer.*

(Other prayers may be added here, ending with: God of mercy: **C:** *Hear our prayer.*)
P: Risen Christ: We pray for your blessing and grace upon your church in every place, including the pastors and congregations here in our city, that they may be faithful witnesses of your resurrection to a world in need of hope and love, that only you can give. God of mercy:
C: *Hear our prayer.*

P: Lord of the nations: There are so many needs and troubled places and peoples around the world; where there is war and hatred, injustice, and persecution, poverty, and exploitation, transform the world by granting wisdom to all leaders of nations, that they may govern with peace and justice. God of mercy:
C: *Hear our prayer.*

P: Jesus our great physician: We pray for those who are ill among us in body, mind or soul, especially those whom we name before you now either aloud or in the silence of our hearts: (PAUSE.) God of mercy:
C: *Hear our prayer.*

P: Hear our prayers Lord God, and grant all else that may be in accord with your holy will and purposes; in the name of Jesus our risen Savior and Lord, who taught us how to pray:
ALL: *Our Father... Amen.*

5th Sunday of Easter

Readings: Acts 8:26-40; Psalm 22:25-31; 1 John 4:7-21; John 15:1-8

P: Life-giving God: In humility and devotion we come here to celebrate your presence in our world, our nation and our personal lives. We honor and worship you, O author of life. God of new life:
C: *Have mercy on us.*

P: Life-giving God: We thank you for people like the disciple Philip, who was led by the Spirit to share the good news of Jesus Christ with the Ethiopian eunuch. Lead us, Spirit of God, that we too may be eager and willing witnesses of Jesus Christ; enable us to be more supportive of mission work and evangelism in your church. God of new life:
C: *Have mercy on us.*

P: Life-giving God: You are pure love and love comes from you. We are most grateful that you sent your son Jesus into the world to be our atoning sacrifice for our sins. You have revealed your love for us through him, and you have promised that if we love one another, you live in us, and your love is perfected in us, for perfect love casts out all fear. God of new life:
C: *Have mercy on us.*

P: Life-giving God: You are our vine grower. We need your nurturing and pruning if we are going to bear fruit. Christ

Praying the Lectionary

our true vine, without you we can do nothing. Prune our selfishness, pride, sin, and every other hindrance that prevents us from bearing fruit. God of new life:
C: *Have mercy on us.*

(Other intercessions and thanksgivings may be included here, ending with: God of new life: **C:** *Have mercy on us.*)

P: Life-giving God: Pour out your immeasurable grace to the leaders and people of our nation and every nation. Guide and inspire us all to care for those who live in poverty and suffer from injustices we pray; that peace with justice, freedom and democracy may prevail in every land. God of new life:
C: *Have mercy on us.*

P: Life-giving God: We remember all among us who suffer from illnesses of mind, body or soul, especially we remember, (NAMES.) God of new life:
C: *Have mercy on us.*

P: Life-giving God: Your church is comprised of many branches, mold and shape us in such a way that we might all benefit from the richness of these many branches. Help us to abide in you, O Christ our vine, that we may also abide more closely in one another. God of new life:
C: *Have mercy on us.*

P: We go into the world knowing that our abiding and risen Christ is with us; in his name we pray.
ALL: *Amen.*

6th Sunday of Easter

Readings: Acts 10:44-48; Psalm 98; 1 John 5:1-6; John 15:9-17

P: God of Israel and the Gentiles: We praise and thank you that you show no partiality, but have poured out your Holy Spirit to people of every nation as they respond to the ministry of word and sacrament. May your Spirit continue to be poured out upon us, that we may love and serve you faithfully all the days of our life, like Peter the apostle. God of mercy:
C: *Hear our prayer.*

P: Heavenly king: You have done marvelous things and we break forth into joyous song, singing your praises. You have given us your steadfast love and faithfulness. You judge the world with righteousness and your peoples with equity. God of mercy:
C: *Hear our prayer.*

P: Loving God: With the work of the Holy Spirit, we are able to believe that Jesus is the Christ. In response to his sacrificial love for us and the victory that he won through his death and resurrection, we are able to obey his commandments, and in faith love God and one another. God of mercy:
C: *Hear our prayer.*

P: Christ our perfect friend: We know and experience you as love. In love you have chosen us, made us your friends;

Praying the Lectionary

and enabled us to love you and one another. By keeping the love commandment, the world, our neighbor and our own lives will be transformed. God of mercy:
C: *Hear our prayer.*

(Additional prayers may be offered here, ending with: God of mercy: **C:** *Hear our prayer.*)

P: Ruler of all nations: Reign over the leaders and people of the world, that the spirit of justice and peace might flow into the hearts, minds, and lives of all people. Guide and equip us to be your effective bearers of justice and peace in the world. God of mercy:
C: *Hear our prayer.*

P: Heavenly parent: We thank you for the countless contributions that our mothers make in our families, in the workplace, in school, and in your church. May you continue to fill them with your all-sufficient grace as they fulfill their divine calling as mothers. God of mercy:
C: *Hear our prayer.*

P: Christ our healer: Today we remember all among us who are sick in body, mind, or spirit; whom we name before you now either aloud or in the silence of our hearts: (PAUSE.) God of mercy:
C: *Hear our prayer.*

P: We thank you, Jesus for being our greatest friend and as we journey into another week, we believe that you have empowered us to love one another as you have loved us. In your holy name we pray.
ALL: *Amen.*

7th Sunday of Easter

Readings: Acts 1:15-17, 21-26; Psalm 1; 1 John 5:9-13; John 17:6-19

P: Holy and eternal God: Your greatness exceeds our wildest hopes and dreams. We are the unworthy inheritors of your amazing grace, and for this you are most worthy of our worship. Life-giving God:
C: *Hear our prayer.*

P: God our righteous judge: May we delight in your law and meditate on it day and night. Number us among the congregation of the righteous, for you watch over the way of the righteous. Life-giving God:
C: *Hear our prayer.*

P: God of truth: We are most grateful for your promise that whoever has the Son has life and those who believe in the name of the son of God may know that they have eternal life. Life-giving God:
C: *Hear our prayer.*

P: Holy, blessed Trinity: As we proclaim your unity and celebrate your diversity, grant that your church might also bear witness to the world as a unified body of Christ while, at the same time, celebrate its rich diversity. Heal the wounds of your church surrounded on all sides by hostility and hatred; help all Christians to work and pray more earnestly for unity in the body of Christ. Life-giving God:

Praying the Lectionary

C: *Hear our prayer.*

(Additional intercessions and thanksgivings may be included here, ending with: Life-giving God: **C:** *Hear our prayer.*)

P: Lord and king: The nations of this world are in a constant state of turmoil and change, war and famine. Bless the leaders and people of every land, that they may draw from your infinite resources to govern responsibly by upholding peace with justice, freedom, and democracy. As your faithful servants in the world, aid us in fulfilling our responsibilities and duties as citizens of this nation and members of the human race. Life-giving God:
C: *Hear our prayer.*

P: Compassionate Christ: We turn to you for the healing of body, mind, and soul for the following persons whom we name either aloud or in the silence of our hearts before you now: (PAUSE.) Life-giving God:
C: *Hear our prayer.*

P: Equipped with your love and inspired by the risen and ascended Christ among us, we go out into another week, sharing your love with one another; we commend these and all other prayers that are in accord with your holy will and purposes, one God, who lives and reigns now and through all ages of ages.
ALL: *Amen.*

Pentecost Sunday

Readings: Acts 2:1-21 or Ezekiel 37:1-14; Psalm 104:24-34, 35b; Romans 8:22-27 or Acts 2:1-21; John 15:26-27, 16:4b-15

P: O Creator-spirit God: You have breathed the breath of life into all creation. May we always praise and thank you for breathing life into us. Hear us as we pray:
C: *Have mercy on us.*

(An alternative congregational response may be to sing the refrain of a Pentecost song, such as "Gracious Spirit, Heed Our Pleading," after each intercession.)

P: O Creator-spirit God: As you spoke through your prophet Ezekiel to the exiled Israelites, giving them new hope in the midst of despair, speak also through your faithful servants today and give your people new hope in the midst of despair. You are the source of hope; help us not to be crushed or defeated by despair. Hear us as we pray:
C: *Have mercy on us.*

P: O Creator-spirit God: We thank you for breathing life into the Christian church. Sustain, sanctify, nurture and guide the church in truth as it continues to be tested and persecuted by the winds of many spirits. Hear us as we pray:
C: *Have mercy on us.*

Praying the Lectionary

P: O Creator-spirit God: As our advocate, you guide and teach us the truth, which is Christ himself. We thank you, Jesus, for giving us your advocate, the Spirit, to help us know you better and walk in your ways. Hear us as we pray:
C: *Have mercy on us.*

(Other prayers may be offered here, ending with: Hear us as we pray: **C:** *Have mercy on us.*)

P: O Creator-spirit God: There are many people in the world who are powerless and forgotten, especially the poor, the refugees, widows and widowers, orphans, the imprisoned and persecuted, the unemployed and underemployed, the sick and shut-in, the countless victims of abuse and injustice. With your presence in our lives, O blessed Spirit, move us to minister compassionately to the world's powerless and forgotten people, whom we take a moment now to remember and name either out loud or in the silence of our hearts: (PAUSE.) Hear us as we pray:
C: *Have mercy on us.*

P: O Creator-spirit God: We pray for Elizabeth our Queen, our Prime Minister and Members of Parliament, our Premier and Members of the Legislative Assembly, (or other appropriate government leaders and titles for other nations may be added here); and the governments of every nation. Bestow on them your wisdom and counsel, that they may govern justly and maintain peace and goodwill among all their citizens, as well as protect and care for the powerless and forgotten. Hear us as we pray:
C: *Have mercy on us.*

Praying the Lectionary

P: Grant us the necessary gifts and fruit "O Holy Spirit" to be your witnesses in the world, as we pray the prayer that Jesus taught us:
ALL: *Our Father… Amen.*

The Holy Trinity Sunday

Readings: Isaiah 6:1-8; Psalm 29; Romans 8:12-17; John 3:1-17

P: God our Creator, redeemer, and sanctifier: We, along with the company of heaven praise you, saying: Holy, holy, holy is the Lord of hosts, the whole earth is full of your glory. Thank you for sending faithful servants like the prophet Isaiah, who confessed his sin and the sin of his people, and they were forgiven in your name. May we willingly serve you and follow the example of Isaiah, who answered your call to him, saying: "Here am I; send me!" God of mercy:
C: *Hear our prayer.*

(An alternative congregational response may be to sing stanza 1 of "Holy, Holy, Holy, Lord God Almighty.")

P: God and king of all creation: You speak and everything in the universe listens and obeys. Your voice is powerful; changing chaos into order; turning death into new life. We are most grateful that you give strength to your people and bless them with your peace. God of mercy:
C: *Hear our prayer.*

(An alternative congregational response may be to sing stanza 2 of "Holy, Holy, Holy, Lord God Almighty.")

P: Blessed Holy Trinity: We thank you that your Spirit of holiness is a dynamic and living power, working in the

Praying the Lectionary

lives of people whenever the gospel is preached and the sacraments are administered. Come Spirit of God, work in the Christian church today: convict us of our sins, correct us when we err, unite us and bestow within us a greater commitment and faith. God of mercy:

C: *Hear our prayer.*

(An alternative congregational response may be to sing stanza 3 of "Holy, Holy, Holy, Lord God Almighty.")

P: Jesus our Savior: Your love is so lofty that it not only includes us, but extends out into the whole world. Great redeemer, prevent us from spurning the costliest gift of all, your love. In baptism you adopted us as heirs of your realm and co-workers with you. The in-breaking of your kingdom becomes a present reality whenever we share faith with the doubter, hope with the hopeless; love with the one who hates, and peace with the one who is violent and at war. God of mercy:

C: *Hear our prayer.*

(An alternative congregational response may be to sing stanza 4 of "Holy, Holy, Holy, Lord God Almighty.")

(Other intercessions and thanksgivings may be added here, ending with: God of mercy: **C:** *Hear our prayer.*)

P: Healing God: We pray for all among us who are suffering from illnesses of the body, mind or spirit; whom we name now before you either aloud or in the silence of our hearts: (PAUSE.) God of mercy:

C: *Hear our prayer.*

Praying the Lectionary

(An alternative congregational response may be to sing stanza 1 of "Holy, Holy, Holy, Lord God Almighty.")

P: God of all people: We pray that you would pour out your wisdom and grace upon all our leaders and the leaders of every nation; help them uphold the rule of law and order, govern responsibly by protecting the weakest and most vulnerable among them, and ensure that peace and justice, freedom, and democracy are preserved. God of mercy:
C: *Hear our prayer.*

(An alternative congregational response may be to sing stanza 2 of "Holy, Holy, Holy, Lord God Almighty.")

P: We commend all of these prayers and whatever else may be proper and wholesome for us to the one, true God, who lives and reigns eternally as the Father, Son, and Holy Spirit.
ALL: *Amen.*

Pentecost 2

Readings: 1 Samuel 8:4-11, (12-15), 16-20, (11:14-15);
Psalm 138;
2 Corinthians 4:13-5:1; Mark 3:20-35

P: God our king: In ancient times, the people of Israel no longer listened to faithful prophets like Samuel. They no longer worshiped you as their king, rather they forsook your ways and insisted on choosing an earthly king, who led them further away from you and your ways. Help us to worship and serve you as our king. God of grace:
C: *Hear our prayer.*

P: God of steadfast love and faithfulness: We praise and thank you for listening to our prayers and strengthening our souls. You also preserve our life in times of trouble and deliver us from our enemies. God of grace:
C: *Hear our prayer.*

P: God of new life: Our world is tossed to-and-fro and in a constant state of turmoil, yet since we share in the victory of Christ's resurrection, we have hope for today and tomorrow. In our yearning for the things that are unseen and eternal, enable us to share the hope of the resurrection with the whole world. God of grace:
C: *Hear our prayer.*

P: Holy Spirit: Open our hearts and lives to your truth, that we may never confuse the work and person of Jesus with that of Satan. Unite all members of the body of Christ, that

Praying the Lectionary

the work of your realm might prosper and grow as we live under the power of your forgiveness. Protect all faithful Christians from falling prey to the falsehoods of many present-day leaders and organizations; preserve us all in the truth. God of grace:
C: *Hear our prayer.*

(Additional prayers may be included here, ending with: God of grace: **C:** *Hear our prayer.*)

P: Sovereign God: We pray for Elizabeth our Queen, our Prime Minister and Members of Parliament, our Premier and Members of the Legislative Assembly, (or other appropriate government leaders and titles for other nations may be added here), and the leaders of all nations: bestow your wisdom and knowledge upon them, that they may uphold peace and justice in the world. God of grace:
C: *Hear our prayer.*

P: Jesus our great physician: We pray for all among us who are ill in body, mind or soul, especially: (NAMES.) Grant them your healing. God of grace:
C: *Hear our prayer.*

P: As disciples of Jesus, hear our prayers, and shower upon us all things that are right and proper in order to accomplish your holy will, now and always. In your name we pray.
ALL: *Amen.*

Pentecost 3

Readings: 1 Samuel 15:34-16:13; Psalm 20; 2 Corinthians 5:6-10, (11-13), 14-17; Mark 4:26-34

P: All-seeing God: We praise and thank you that in ancient times you led your prophet Samuel, teaching him that you do not see as mortals see; they look on the outward appearance, but you, Lord, look on the heart. Samuel therefore was led by you to anoint David as king over Israel. Help us also to learn not to judge others only by looking at their outward appearance. Loving God:
C: *Have mercy on us.*

P: God our deliverer: As you delivered your people Israel from danger and harm, so you grant victory to us and grant our heart's desire by fulfilling our prayers. May we not take pride in earthly powers, but in the name of the Lord our God. Loving God:
C: *Have mercy on us.*

P: God of our journeys: You have made us a pilgrim people; we live by faith not by sight. Thank you for the gift of faith; support and guide us to walk by faith, particularly when we are tempted to measure our accomplishments by instant results and rewards. Loving God:
C: *Have mercy on us.*

P: Jesus our greatest teacher: Today we are reminded that the kingdom of God is like a tiny mustard seed, growing slowly and quietly into a great shrub. Led by your Spirit,

Praying the Lectionary

move us to share the good news with others, that your kingdom might grow to embrace every single human being in our global village. Loving God:
C: *Have mercy on us.*
(Additional intercessions and thanksgivings may be offered here, ending with: Loving God: **C:** *Have mercy on us.*)

P: Healer of all: We pray for all among us who are ill in body, mind or spirit, especially: (NAMES.) Loving God:
C: *Have mercy on us.*

P: Heavenly Father: Today we remember and pray for all earthly fathers; grant them your grace so that they may be able to provide for their families and serve as faithful, loving, caring role models for their children By doing so, help them to contribute to the over-all stability of society. Loving God:
C: *Have mercy on us.*

P: Ruler of all nations: In this age of computers, genetic engineering and nuclear energy, human beings have the potential for accomplishing much good on this planet. Yet, at the same time, the possibility exists for the human beings to destroy all humankind and planet earth. Rule over the governments and people of all nations; pour out your grace that they may strive for justice and peace throughout the whole world. Loving God:
C: *Have mercy on us.*

P: In mercy, hear our prayer for the sake of Jesus Christ our Savior, Lord, friend, and brother.
ALL: *Amen.*

Pentecost 4

Readings: 1 Samuel 17:(1a, 4-11, 19-23) 32-49 or
1 Samuel 17:57-18:5, 10-16; Psalm 9:9-20 or Psalm 133;
2 Corinthians 6:1-13; Mark 4:35-41

P: Lord of hosts: In ancient times you delivered the Israelites from the Philistines by granting David the courage to defeat Goliath. In times of danger, when we face the battles of life, grant us the courage to place all of our trust in you, Lord God, to deliver us, just as your servant David did long ago. God of mercy:
C: *Hear our prayer.*

P: God our stronghold: We praise and thank you that the needy shall not always be forgotten, nor the hope of the poor perish forever. You are the just judge of all nations, and do not forget the cry of the afflicted. God of mercy:
C: *Hear our prayer.*

P: Gracious God: Pour out your Holy Spirit on us, that we may not accept the grace of God in vain. Help us to make each day count. Now is the acceptable time, now is the day of salvation. God of mercy:
C: *Hear our prayer.*

P: Master of wind and sea: Long ago you were able to exercise your divine power by stopping the wind and quieting the waves. We ask you to be with us, to calm the storms of our lives and bring us your peace. God of mercy:
C: *Hear our prayer.*

Praying the Lectionary

(Other prayers may be included here, ending with: God of mercy: **C:** *Hear our prayer.*)

P: Lord of all nations: Bestow your grace on all the leaders of the nations, including our federal and provincial governments, that they may protect the weakest and most vulnerable of their citizens and ensure that peace and justice prevail. God of mercy:
C: *Hear our prayer.*

P: Christ our healer: We come to you for the healing of body, mind and soul. Especially today, we remember those who we name before you now either aloud or in the silence of our hearts: (NAMES.) God of mercy:
C: *Hear our prayer.*

P: Christ our Good Shepherd: In times of rapid change, bless the mission and ministry of your church around the globe. Pour out the fruit and gifts of your Holy Spirit, that Christians everywhere may do their part to bear faithful witness to you by spreading the gospel in word and action to all people. God of mercy:
C: *Hear our prayer.*

P: Hear our prayers, O God our Father, who together with your son Jesus and the Holy Spirit lives and reigns, one God, now and forever.
ALL: *Amen.*

Pentecost 5

Readings: 2 Samuel 1:1, 17-27; Psalm 130;
2 Corinthians 8:7-15; Mark 5:21-43

P: Heavenly king: Unlike all earthly rulers, you are a God of compassion and have mercy upon your people. We thank you that we, like David of old, can turn to you for comfort and counsel in times of loss and grief. As David poured out his lament over the deaths of Saul and Jonathan, so may we turn to you and pour out our sorrow when we lose our loved ones. God of grace:
C: *Your mercy is great.*

P: Merciful Lord: You have promised to hear our supplications; so we cry out to you, seeking your forgiveness. In you we place our hope, your steadfast love and power to redeem are our constant strength. God of grace:
C: *Your mercy is great.*

P: Loving God: Thanks to Jesus, you have shown us how to love. In our abundance, may we be eager to share with others in need, so that in their abundance they may be eager to share with us in our time of need. In this way, the one that has much does not have too much, and the one who has little does not have too little. God of grace:
C: *Your mercy is great.*

P: Christ our healer: Long ago you healed Jairus' daughter and a woman who had suffered from hemorrhages for twelve years. We pray for all who are ill and in need of

Praying the Lectionary

healing, whether it be mental, emotional, physical or spiritual; we name them now before you either out loud or in the silence of our hearts: (NAMES.) God of grace:
C: *Your mercy is great.*

(Additional intercessions and thanksgivings may be offered here, ending with: God of grace: **C:** *Your mercy is great.*)

P: Lord of the church: We pray for your blessing upon all Christians and churches, that the gospel would be shared around the globe in thought, word, and action. God of grace:
C: *Your mercy is great.*

P: God of all nations: We remember Elizabeth our Queen, our Prime Minister and Members of Parliament, our Premier and Members of the Legislative Assembly, (or other appropriate government leaders and titles for other nations may be added here) and the leaders of every nation. Pour out your grace upon them, that justice and peace may prevail in every land. God of grace:
C: *Your mercy is great.*

P: Into your all-sufficient hands we commend all for whom we pray, trusting in your mercy, through Jesus Christ our Savior and Lord.
ALL: *Amen.*

Pentecost 6

Readings: 2 Samuel 5:1-5, 9-10; Psalm 48; 2 Corinthians 12:2-10; Mark 6:1-13

P: Heavenly king: In ancient times you blessed David as king over Judah and Israel, giving him gifts and skills to lead your chosen people. We praise and thank you for all leaders who you call and bless to lead your people today in the way of justice and peace. God of mercy:
C: *Hear our prayer.*

P: Lord of hosts: You are greatly to be praised for your steadfast love. Your name, O God, like your praise, reaches the ends of the Earth. Your right hand is filled with victory. God of mercy:
C: *Hear our prayer.*

P: Gracious God: As the apostle Paul learned, so may we learn that your grace is sufficient for us, for power is made perfect in weakness. For your sake, O Christ, help us to faithfully bear our sufferings, for whenever we are weak, then we are strong. God of mercy:
C: *Hear our prayer.*

P: Jesus our teacher and head of the church: We thank you for calling your disciples to a ministry of preaching the gospel and healing the sick in body, mind, and soul. We pray for all whom you call today, to a ministry of preaching the gospel and healing the sick. Bless them as they endeavor to be your faithful servants. We also remember

Praying the Lectionary

those among us who are ill in mind, body or spirit, especially those whom we name before you now either aloud or in the silence of our hearts: (NAMES.) God of mercy:
C: *Hear our prayer.*
(Additional prayers may be included here, ending with: God of mercy: **C:** *Hear our prayer.*)

P: Sovereign God: We pray for Elizabeth our Queen, our Prime Minister and Members of Parliament, our Premier and Members of the Legislative Assembly, (or other appropriate government leaders and titles for other nations may be added here), and all heads of state in every nation. Pour out the wisdom and truth of your Holy Spirit, that they may govern their citizens by upholding the rule of law and order, and striving for peace and justice for all people. God of mercy:
C: *Hear our prayer.*

P: We pray that you would hear our prayers, and grant us all that is wholesome and proper, as we pray the prayer Jesus taught us:
ALL: *Our Father.... Amen.*

Pentecost 7

Readings: Amos 7:7-15; Psalm 85:8-13; Ephesians 1:3-14; Mark 6:14-29

P: God of Amos and the Israelite prophets: We praise and thank you for calling the prophets of every time and place to speak your word of truth to the worldly powers. Open our hearts and minds to the truth of your prophetic word as it speaks to us today, that we may listen and act in accord with your will and purposes. God of mercy:
C: *Hear our prayer.*

P: Righteous God: We are most grateful that you have showered upon us your steadfast love and faithfulness, your righteousness and peace. May we never take these divine blessings for granted; in order that they may be deeply embedded within us and our daily living. God of mercy:
C: *Hear our prayer.*

P: Gracious God: You are blessed, and from you come blessings upon blessings. In Christ we are given every spiritual blessing; you have chosen and adopted us in Christ. We have redemption through Christ's blood and the forgiveness of our trespasses, according to the riches of his grace that he lavished on us. God of mercy:
C: *Hear our prayer.*

P: Christ our suffering servant: John the baptizer went ahead of you to prepare your way. His life and death were

Praying the Lectionary

foreshadowing of your life and death. John, like you, spoke truthfully to the worldly powers and suffered the consequences. John, like you, reminds us that the kingdoms of this world and your kingdom are in constant conflict with one another. Today we remember all of the Christian martyrs who, like you and John, were prepared to sacrifice their lives for the sake of the truth of your gospel kingdom. Today we also pray for our brothers and sisters in Christ, who are being persecuted in nations hostile to you and the Christian faith. Provide for their needs in every way and grant them courage to keep their faith as they witness your gospel truth. We ask that your Holy Spirit would strengthen our resolve to be witnesses to your kingdom coming in the world today. God of mercy:
C: *Hear our prayer.*

(Other prayers may be added here, ending with: God of mercy: **C:** *Hear our prayer.*)

P: Christ our great physician: Today we remember all those among us who are ill in body, mind or soul, especially those whom we name either aloud or in the silence of our hearts before you now: (NAMES.) God of mercy:
C: *Hear our prayer.*

P: Sovereign king: We remember all worldly leaders who have authority to govern in our nation and every other nation. Pour out upon them your Spirit's gifts and fruit, that they may rule their citizens by upholding justice and peace, freedom and democracy. God of mercy:
C: *Hear our prayer.*

Praying the Lectionary

P: Hear our prayers, both spoken and unspoken for the sake of Jesus our Lord and Savior, who lives and reigns with you and the Holy Spirit, one God, now and through all ages of ages.
ALL: *Amen.*

Pentecost 8

Readings: 2 Samuel 7:1-14a; Psalm 89:20-37; Ephesians 2:11-22; Mark 6:30-34, 53-56

P: Lord of hosts: We praise and thank you that long ago, you promised your servant David an everlasting kingdom. In the fullness of time, you sent your Son, Jesus the Messiah, from the line of David to fulfill your promise of an everlasting kingdom, and that we would be members of it. God of grace:
C: *Hear our prayer.*

P: Covenant-making God: We are most grateful that your steadfast love and faithfulness are never-ending. In times of hardship and trouble, we tend to forget that we can cry to you for help; you are our Father, our God, and the rock of our salvation. God of grace:
C: *Hear our prayer.*

P: Loving God: In Christ we have been brought near to you by his blood. He is our peace, he has broken down the dividing wall of hostility between Jew and Gentile, slave and free, male and female. He has reconciled us through the saving power of his cross; through him we have access in one Spirit to the Father. We are filled with gratitude that we are now citizens of the household of God; help us to carry out the ministry of reconciliation in the church and the world. God of grace:
C: *Hear our prayer.*

Praying the Lectionary

P: Christ our great physician: You had compassion on the crowds who came to you from far and wide, bringing with them those in need of healing of body, mind, and spirit. So too do we come before you today, and ask for your healing presence and power for those whom we name either out loud or in the silence of our hearts before you now: (PAUSE.) God of grace:
C: *Hear our prayer.*

(Other intercessions and thanksgivings may be included here, ending with: God of grace: **C:** *Hear our prayer.*)

P: Lord of all nations: We pray for the leaders of every nation, including our own, especially Elizabeth our Queen, our Prime Minister and Members of Parliament, our Premier and Members of the Legislative Assembly, (or other appropriate government leaders and titles for other nations may be added here) our mayor and city council; grant them wisdom and discernment to maintain peace and justice, freedom and democracy. God of grace:
C: *Hear our prayer.*

P: Jesus the Good Shepherd: We pray for your church around the world and here in our nation, that you would continue to bless its mission and ministry in every place. God of grace:
C: *Hear our prayer.*

P: All of these prayers and anything else that may be in accord with your holy will and purposes, grant as we pray in the name of Jesus our Lord and Savior.
ALL: *Amen.*

Pentecost 9

Readings: 2 Samuel 11:1-15; Psalm 14; Ephesians 3:14-21; John 6:1-21

P: God of love: We praise and thank you, for you have given us your gift of love, a love that is to be shared in our relationships. Help us to be loving and faithful especially in our relationships within our family as husbands and wives, parents and children. Hear us as we pray:
C: *Have mercy on us.*

P: God of love: You are with the company of the righteous; you are the refuge of the poor. Grant us your compassion, that we may walk with the poor and minister to their needs. Hear us as we pray:
C: *Have mercy on us.*

P: God of love: Strengthen our inner being with power through your Spirit, that Christ may dwell in our hearts through faith, as we are being rooted and grounded in love. Hear us as we pray:
C: *Have mercy on us.*

P: God of love: Today, Jesus, we learn how generously you provide for our needs. Remind us to trust that you not only provide for our earthly needs, but you feed us abundantly with the heavenly food of word and sacrament, which equips us to become more mature Christians. Hear us as we pray:
C: *Have mercy on us.*

Praying the Lectionary

(Additional prayers may be offered here, ending with: Hear us as we pray: **C:** *Have mercy on us.*)

P: God of love: You invite us to pray for those who are ill in body, mind or spirit, we especially today remember: NAMES, and those who we name either aloud or silently before you now: (PAUSE.) Hear us as we pray:
C: *Have mercy on us.*

P: God of love: We pray for peace and goodwill among all the nations and leaders of nations — bestow on them your wisdom and counsel in the way of truth. Hear us as we pray:
C: *Have mercy on us.*

P: In response to your abundance, Lord Jesus, give us a spirit of generosity toward you and other people, especially the poor, the sick, the hungry, the refugees, the widows, widowers, and orphans, and all who are weighed down with great suffering or persecution. We pray this in your holy name.
ALL: *Amen.*

Pentecost 10

Readings: 2 Samuel 11:26-12:13a; Psalm 51:1-12; Ephesians 4:1-16; John 6:24-35

P: Holy and righteous God: Long ago you sent prophets like Nathan to speak the truth to King David and expose his sins against you. In our day, we praise and thank you for sending prophets who speak the truth to those in places of power and expose their sins. Bestow your grace upon all of your people, that we may follow your ways. God of mercy:
C: *Hear our prayer.*

P: Merciful Lord: We thank and praise you for showing mercy on us, according to your steadfast love. Wash us thoroughly from our iniquity and cleanse us from our sin. We know our transgressions, and our sin is ever before us. Create in us clean hearts, O God, and renew a right spirit within us. Do not cast us away from your presence, and do not take your Holy Spirit from us. Restore to us the joy of your salvation and uphold us with a willing spirit. God of mercy:
C: *Hear our prayer.*

P: Loving God: Your Holy Spirit has given us a variety of gifts to preserve the unity of the church. Grant us those gifts that we may speak the truth in love, and grow up in every way into Christ who is the head, from whom the whole body, joined and knit together by every ligament with which it is equipped, as each part is working prop-

erly promotes the body's growth in building itself up in love. God of mercy:
C: *Hear our prayer.*

P: Christ, the Bread of Life: You have given us the promise to fill us with the food that never perishes, the food that endures for eternal life. In a world full of people that do not have enough to eat and drink, help us to be more generous in sharing our resources with the poor. Beyond our physical need for food and drink, you feed us with the spiritual food and drink through the sacrament of Holy Communion. We thank you for this heavenly food and drink, which draws us closer to you. God of mercy:
C: *Hear our prayer.*

(Additional thanksgivings and intercessions may be included here, ending with: God of mercy: **C:** *Hear our prayer.*)

P: Christ our healer: Today we remember those who are ill among us in body, mind, or spirit, especially: (NAMES.) God of mercy:
C: *Hear our prayer.*

P: Lord of all nations: We pray for all heads of state, especially Elizabeth our Queen, our Prime Minister and Members of Parliament, our Premier and Members of the Legislative Assembly, (or other appropriate government leaders and titles for other nations may be added here) our mayor and city council. Grant them your grace to govern by upholding the weakest and most vulnerable among them, that justice and peace may prevail in every land. God of mercy:

Praying the Lectionary

C: *Hear our prayer.*

P: Into your all-sufficient hands we commend all for whom we pray, most merciful God, Father, Son, and Holy Spirit, who lives and reigns now and forever.
ALL: *Amen.*

Pentecost 11

Readings: 2 Samuel 18:5-9, 15, 31-33; Psalm 130; Ephesians 4:25-5:2; John 6:35, 41-51

P: Heavenly Father: We praise and thank you for your parental love that you so generously pour out upon us. You have created us to live within our family and to love one another. We too are grieved like King David whenever death tragically takes a child from us. We pray for all parents who have lost a child; grant them your comfort and healing. Loving God:
C: *Hear our prayer.*

P: Great redeemer: We, like the psalmist can, out of the depths cry to you. You hear our voice and supplications. Your steadfast love and forgiveness have the power to redeem us. You are our hope, now and forever. Loving God:
C: *Hear our prayer.*

P: Compassionate Christ: Your love for us is like a fragrant offering and sacrifice to God. In response to your love for us, help us not to grieve the Holy Spirit. Rather, may we become imitators of God as beloved children, living in love. Loving God:
C: *Hear our prayer.*

P: Jesus Bread of Life: We cannot live without physical bread to feed and keep our bodies healthy. You have made us for yourself, so that we cannot spiritually live without you; you are the Bread of Life. Whoever comes to you will

Praying the Lectionary

never be hungry, and whoever believes in you will never be thirsty. Thank you for the sacrament of Holy Communion which strengthens our faith, cleanses us of sin, and offers healing of the mind, body, and soul. Loving God:
C: *Hear our prayer.*
(Other prayers may be added here, ending with: Loving God: **C:** *Hear our prayer.*)

P: Jesus our great physician: We pray for all among us who are ill in body, mind or spirit, especially: (NAMES.) Loving God:
C: *Hear our prayer.*

P: Divine sovereign: Rule with your perfect justice and peace in every land. We pray for peace with justice, for reconciliation between enemies; for the forgotten, the poor, the persecuted, those unjustly imprisoned and tortured, for the unemployed and underemployed, for the lonely and depressed, for widows, widowers and orphans, for the young and the old. Loving God:
C: *Hear our prayer.*

P: Hear our prayers, God of mercy, and whatever else may be proper and wholesome, grant for the sake of Christ our Lord and Savior, who lives and reigns with you and the Holy Spirit; one God, now and forever.
ALL: *Amen.*

Pentecost 12

Readings: 1 Kings 2:10-12; 3:3-14; Psalm 111; Ephesians 5:15-20; John 6:51-58

P: Heavenly King: We praise and thank you for ruling over your people with your steadfast love, and that you hear our prayers. You blessed King Solomon with a wise and discerning mind to lead your people according to your ways. Grant all earthly leaders your wisdom and a discerning mind, that they may lead your people today according to your will. God of mercy:
C: *Hear our prayer.*

P: Righteous God: We worship you, for you are gracious and merciful, providing food for those who fear you; ever mindful of your covenant. The works of your hands are faithful and just, sending redemption to your people. God of mercy:
C: *Hear our prayer.*

P: God of time and eternity: Help us to live as wise people, making the most of our time, that we may understand the will of the Lord. Fill us with the Holy Spirit as we sing psalms, hymns and spiritual songs and make melody to the Lord. God of mercy:
C: *Hear our prayer.*

P: Christ our living bread: You have given us the promise that through participating in the sacrament of Holy Communion, we will abide in you and you in us and we will

Praying the Lectionary

have eternal life. God of mercy:
C: *Hear our prayer.*

(Other intercessions and thanksgivings may be included here, ending with: God of mercy: **C:** *Hear our prayer.*)
P: Christ our healer: In compassion for the human race, you offer healing of body, mind, and spirit; therefore we pray for all among us who are ill, those whom we name either aloud or in the silence of our hearts before you now: (PAUSE.) God of mercy:
C: *Hear our prayer.*

P: In your mercy, hear our prayers and grant all else that may be in accord with your holy will and purposes, O God, Father, Son, and Holy Spirit, who lives and reigns now and forever.
ALL: *Amen.*

Pentecost 13

Readings: 1 Kings 8:(1, 6, 10-11) 22-30, 41-43; Psalm 84; Ephesians 6:10-20; John 6:56-69

P: Lord God of Israel and the Gentiles: In the days of King Solomon, you blessed your people and heard their prayers as they worshiped you in the Jerusalem temple. We too worship you here in this place and turn to you in prayer, trusting that you hear us. God of mercy:
C: *Hear our prayer.*

P: Lord of hosts: Our souls long, indeed faint, for the courts of your dwelling place, as we sing for joy to you the living God. Happy are those who live in your house, ever singing your praise; for a day in your courts is better than a thousand elsewhere. God of mercy:
C: *Hear our prayer.*

P: Almighty God: Only in you do we find the strength by putting on the whole armor of God to wage battle against the wiles of the devil and all other powers of evil. Bestow your Spirit upon us, that we may take up the whole armor of God, to stand firm in the faith by trusting in the saving power of your word and persevering in prayer. God of mercy:
C: *Hear our prayer.*

P: Christ the bread that came down from heaven: We are filled with gratitude that you have promised we will live forever if we partake of you, the bread of heaven. In

Praying the Lectionary

a world that is full of competing forces to draw us away from you, may we, like the apostle Peter say: "Lord, to whom can we go? You have the words of eternal life. We have come to believe and know that you are the Holy one of God." God of mercy:
C: *Hear our prayer.*

(Additional prayers may be offered here, ending with: God of mercy: **C:** *Hear our prayer.*)

P: Jesus our great physician: Today we turn to you for healing of body, mind, and soul; we especially pray for: (NAMES.) God of mercy:
C: *Hear our prayer.*

P: God our king: The world is full of injustice, suffering, divisions, strife, wars, and rumors; instill within the hearts, minds and lives of the nations' leaders, your wisdom to govern by working for and preserving peace and justice in every land. God of mercy:
C: *Hear our prayer.*

P: Hear us as we commend our prayers into your all-sufficient hands, even as we pray:
ALL: *Our Father.... Amen.*

Pentecost 14

Readings: Song of Solomon 2:8-13; Psalm 45:1-2, 6-9; James 1:17-27; Mark 7:1-8, 14-15, 21-23

P: God of love: We praise and thank you for creating love in our hearts and giving us countless blessings through the gift of marriage and the family, both by blood and through you. In all of our family relationships, may our love for one another reflect the love you have given us. God of grace:
C: *Have mercy on us.*

P: Divine sovereign: Your throne, O God, endures forever and ever. Your royal scepter is a scepter of equity; you love righteousness and hate wickedness. May the oil of gladness overflow from our hearts as we worship you. God of grace:
C: *Have mercy on us.*

P: Father of orphans, widows, and widowers: You have taught us that true religion is more than words and rituals. Religion pure and undefiled is this: to care for orphans and widows in their distress, and to keep oneself unstained by the world. Bestow your Spirit upon us in this way, that we may put your word into practical living. God of grace:
C: *Have mercy on us.*

P: Loving Messiah: You have taught us that external rituals may not purify us if our hearts are far from you. You also taught us that all evil intentions come from the hu-

man heart. Please grant us clean hearts and a right spirit, that we may worship and serve you in ways that honor you. God of grace:
C: *Have mercy on us.*

(Additional intercessions and thanksgivings may be included here, ending with: God of grace: **C:** *Have mercy on us.*)

P: Healing Savior: Today we remember all among us who are ill in body, mind or spirit, especially: (NAMES.) God of grace:
C: *Have mercy on us.*

P: Lord of the church: We remember your whole church on earth; continue to bless all Christians with your grace and the gifts and fruit of the Holy Spirit; that your church would grow in numbers and in a deeper commitment to you. God of grace:
C: *Have mercy on us.*

P: God of Israel and the Gentiles: Pour out your wisdom upon Elizabeth our Queen, our Prime Minister and Members of Parliament, our Premier and Members of the Legislative Assembly, (or other appropriate government leaders and titles for other nations may be added here) and the governments of every land, that they may respect and uphold the most vulnerable citizens and ensure that peace and justice prevails everywhere. God of grace:
C: *Have mercy on us.*

Praying the Lectionary

P: Into your all-sufficient hands we commend our prayers and all else that may be in accord with your holy will and purposes; in the name of Jesus our Savior and Lord.
ALL: *Amen.*

Pentecost 15

Readings: Proverbs 22:1-2, 8-9, 22-23; Psalm 125; James 2:1-10 (11-13) 14-17; Mark 7:24-37

P: Maker of heaven and earth: We worship you, as you provide wisdom to live a life that is pleasing to you. Bless us with the gift of generosity that we may share our bread with the poor and sow the seeds of justice among them. God of mercy:
C: *Hear our prayer.*

P: God of peace: You go to those who are good, those who are upright in their hearts. We ask you to surround your people with peace in our hearts, in the church, and in the world. God of mercy:
C: *Hear our prayer.*

P: Jesus our righteous judge: Remind us that God has chosen the poor in the world to be rich in faith, and to be heirs of the promised kingdom to those who love Him. In honoring and caring for the poor, we honor and care for you. Help us to love our neighbor as we love ourselves, especially those who are poor. God of mercy:
C: *Hear our prayer.*

P: Compassionate Savior: Long ago, you healed the Syrophoenician's little daughter of an unclean spirit and a man who was deaf and could not speak. We pray that your ministry of healing would continue among us too, as

we pray for all who are sick in body, mind, or soul, especially: (NAMES.) God of mercy:
C: *Hear our prayer.*

(Other prayers may be added here, ending with: God of mercy: **C:** *Hear our prayer.*)

P: Lord of the church: We pray for your blessing upon all leaders, bishops, pastors, and chaplains; may you grant them your grace to faithfully serve you and your people. God of mercy:
C: *Hear our prayer.*

P: God of all nations: Bestow your wisdom and compassion on Elizabeth our Queen, our Prime Minister and Members of Parliament, our Premier and Members of the Legislative Assembly, (or other appropriate government leaders and titles for other nations may be added here) and the governments of every land, that peace with justice, freedom and democracy would be upheld in every country. God of mercy:
C: *Hear our prayer.*

P: Hear these our prayers and grant whatever else may serve your holy will and purposes, O God, Father, Son, and Holy Spirit, who lives and reigns now and through all ages of ages.
ALL: *Amen.*

Pentecost 16

Readings: Proverbs 1:20-33; Psalm 19; James 3:1-12; Mark 8:27-38

P: All-wise God: We praise and thank you for the gifts of knowledge, wisdom and counsel. May we choose the fear of the Lord, so that we may gain knowledge, wisdom and counsel; for you have promised that those who listen to you will be secure and will live at ease, without dread or disaster. Hear us, Lord, as we pray:
C: *Have mercy on us.*

P: God of all creation: The heavens are telling the glory of God; heaven's vault makes known his handiwork. The law of the Lord is perfect and revives the soul. The Lord's instruction never fails, it makes the simple wise. May we desire them more than pure gold, for they are sweeter than honey dripping from the honeycomb. Hear us, Lord, as we pray:
C: *Have mercy on us.*

P: God of the word and speech: We thank you for giving us human beings lips, mouths, tongues, and voices, the word and speech. Even though a bridle can control and turn or stop a horse and a small rudder can steer a large ship, the tongue is almost impossible to control. We pray that you forgive us for all of the sinful and hurtful words that our tongues speak. Forgive us, control our tongues, and help us to employ them to praise you and speak words of love and kindness to one another. Hear us, Lord, as we pray:

Praying the Lectionary

C: *Have mercy on us.*

P: Jesus our cross-bearing Messiah: How hard it is to hear your words about sacrifice, suffering, denying of self and death by crucifixion! Forgive us when we, like the apostle Peter, confess you as the Messiah one moment, and then the next moment wish to avoid following you in the way of the cross. Pour out your Spirit upon us, that we may be your followers by denying ourselves and taking up our crosses to follow wherever you lead us. Hear us, Lord, as we pray:
C: *Have mercy on us.*

(Other intercessions and thanksgivings may be included here, ending with: Hear us Lord as we pray: **C:** *Have mercy on us.*)

P: Christ our great physician: You have the power and love to heal us; we pray for all among us who suffer physically, mentally, and spiritually, especially: (NAMES.) Hear us, Lord, as we pray:
C: *Have mercy on us.*

P: Merciful Savior: We pray for your church around the world and here at home, that you would bestow the gifts and fruit of your Holy Spirit upon all Christians to live in love and unity with one another and faithfully bear witness to the gospel in the world. Hear us, Lord, as we pray:
C: *Have mercy on us.*

P: Mighty king: We pray for the leaders of this nation and of every nation, that you would grant them the gifts of

Praying the Lectionary

wisdom, knowledge, and counsel to govern their citizens with justice, peace, and protect the most vulnerable among them. Hear us, Lord, as we pray:
C: *Have mercy on us.*

P: Hear our prayers and have mercy on us, O God, Father, Son, and Holy Spirit as you live and reign over us, now and forever.
ALL: *Amen.*

Pentecost 17

Readings: Proverbs 31:10-31; Psalm 1; James 3:13-4:3, 7-8a;Mark 9:30-37

P: Ancient of days: We praise and thank you for all the blessings you so generously shower upon us from day-to-day. We especially thank you for the institution of marriage and the family, and for all of the contributions that faithful wives and mothers make to enrich family life. You have told us that charm is deceitful and beauty is vain, but a woman who fears the Lord is to be praised. Bless all women who are faithful to you. God of love:
C: *Hear our prayer.*

P: God of wisdom: Happy are those who delight in your holy ways. They are like trees planted by streams of water, which yield their fruit in its season, and their leaves do not wither. In all they do, they prosper. We thank you Lord, for watching over the way of the righteous. God of love:
C: *Hear our prayer.*

P: God of all nations: In your wisdom you scrutinize the innermost thoughts and motives of every living creature. All evil plots and schemes stand under the judgement of your righteousness. There are many places in the world that are scandalized and victimized by war and oppression. Send out your peacemakers to every corner of the globe, that all nations might walk in your ways of justice and peace. God of love:
C: *Hear our prayer.*

Praying the Lectionary

P: Jesus our loving Savior: We thank you for your life-giving death on the cross and your death-shattering resurrection. In our faith journey, teach us to be like children, that we may rely on you for strength, guidance and understanding. Forgive us, O Christ, for deceitfully believing that we do not need you in our lives. God of love:
C: *Hear our prayer.*

(Additional prayers may be offered here, ending with: God of love: **C:** *Hear our prayer.*)

P: Healing Savior: Today we remember all among us who are ill and suffering in body, mind, or spirit, especially: (NAMES.) God of love:
C: *Hear our prayer.*

P: We entrust our prayers, our hearts, minds, and lives and all things into your tender loving care, in the holy name of Jesus.
ALL: *Amen.*

Pentecost 18

Readings: Esther 7:1-6, 9-10; 9:20-22; Psalm 124; James 5:13-20; Mark 9:38-50

P: God of Israel and all nations: We praise and thank you for people of faith and courage like Esther and Mordecai, who were able to take bold actions in order to ensure the protection and survival of their people. Grant us faith and courage like Esther and Mordecai to help those who are vulnerable and in danger. God of mercy;
C: *Hear our prayer.*

P: God our defender: We, like your people in ancient times, are most grateful that our help is in the name of the Lord, who made heaven and earth, who delivers us from our enemies. God of mercy;
C: *Hear our prayer.*

P: Healing Lord: You have instructed us to care for the sick by calling together the faithful to pray and anoint them with oil. You have given your promise that the prayer of faith will save the sick, and you will lift them up, and anyone who has committed sins and confessed them will be forgiven them and be healed. The prayer of the righteous is powerful and effective. So it is in that spirit of prayer that we come before you now and pray for all among us who are sick in body, mind, or spirit, whom we name aloud or in the silence of our hearts: (NAMES.) God of mercy;
C: *Hear our prayer.*

Praying the Lectionary

P: Jesus our greatest teacher: We thank you for your teachings, which always give us a new perspective on life, its meaning and purpose. You have said that we shall be rewarded even for the smallest acts of kindness and love, like giving a cup of water to someone who is thirsty, and protecting children from danger or harm. God of mercy;
C: *Hear our prayer.*

(Additional intercessions and thanksgivings may be included here, ending with: God of mercy; **C:** *Hear our prayer.*)

P: Compassionate Savior: We pray for your blessings upon all Christians; we remember our brothers and sisters in Christ who suffer from persecution and torture, we pray for the children, teenagers and young adults in the church; protect them from all danger and harm and grant them a deep hunger and thirst for your righteousness. Grant your Holy Spirit's gifts and fruit to every Christian, that they may walk in your ways and bear witness to you and the gospel. God of mercy;
C: *Hear our prayer.*

P: Ruler of all: Pour out your wisdom and grace upon the leaders of every nation, that they may govern their peoples with justice and peace. God of mercy;
C: *Hear our prayer.*

P: Into your merciful hands we commend all for whom we pray, trusting in your all-sufficient grace O Christ, our Lord and Savior.
ALL: *Amen.*

Pentecost 19

Readings: Job 1:1; 2:1-10; Psalm 26; Hebrews 1:1-4; 2:5-12; Mark10:2-16

P: God of heaven and earth: You gave your servant Job the capacity to be blameless and upright, to fear you and turn away from evil. Grant us your grace to learn from the example of your servant Job, that we too may remain loyal to you and your ways regardless of our circumstances. Lord, hear us as we pray:
C: *Have mercy on us.*

P: Blessed Lord: We praise and thank you for your steadfast love, which helps us to walk in faithfulness to you. We sing aloud a song of thanksgiving and tell all your wondrous deeds. Help our feet to stand on level ground; in the great congregation we will bless you. Lord, hear us as we pray:
C: *Have mercy on us.*

P: Ancient of days: We thank you, that long ago you spoke to our ancestors in many and various ways by the prophets, but in these last days you have spoken to us by your son, Jesus. He is the reflection of your glory and the exact imprint of your being, he sustains all things by his powerful word. We are most grateful that you made Jesus, the pioneer of our salvation, perfect through sufferings. Lord, hear us as we pray:
C: *Have mercy on us.*

Praying the Lectionary

P: Jesus lover of children: When your disciples spoke sternly to children and tried to send them away, you became indignant and invited the children to come to you, saying that the kingdom of God belongs to children, and teaching us that we need to receive and enter the kingdom of God as a little child. Grant us hearts of tenderness and love for all of your children, realizing that they are precious in your sight and that they are most welcome in our midst. Lord, hear us as we pray:
C: *Have mercy on us.*

(Other prayers may be added here, ending with: Lord, hear us as we pray: **C:** *Have mercy on us.*)

P: Jesus our great physician: We pray for all among us who are ill in body, mind or spirit, especially: (NAMES.) Lord, hear us as we pray:
C: *Have mercy on us.*

P: Lord of all peoples: Pour out your wisdom upon the leaders of every nation, including Elizabeth our Queen, our Prime Minister and Members of Parliament, our Premier and Members of the Legislative Assembly, (or other appropriate government leaders and titles for other nations may be added here) that they may govern by administering the rule of law with justice and peace, as well as defend the weak and forgotten. Lord, hear us as we pray:
C: *Have mercy on us.*

P: Jesus our Messiah: We pray for your church here and around the globe, that you would pour out your Spirit's gifts and fruit upon us all, that we may live in unity as

Praying the Lectionary

we love and serve one another, and care for your creation. Lord, hear us as we pray:
C: *Have mercy on us.*

P: All of these prayers and whatever else may be in accord with your holy will and purposes we commend to you, O Triune God, who lives and reigns through all ages of ages.
ALL: *Amen.*

Pentecost 20

Readings: Job 23:1-9, 16-17; Psalm 22:1-15; Hebrews 4:12-16; Mark 10:17-31

P: Holy one of heaven and earth: We praise and thank you for teaching us that your actions are not always meant to be understood by us; you have your reasons for everything even though we are not able to comprehend them. We confess sometimes that we, like Job, find it difficult to wait on you and feel that you are absent from us at times. In times of trouble and loneliness, help us to remain faithful to you. God of grace:
C: *Have mercy on us.*

P: Lord our deliverer: In times of suffering, we have moments like the psalmist when we feel forsaken, and our prayers and cries for help go unanswered. However, we do know that your faithfulness has been constant and your people in every generation trusted in you to deliver them. May we too place all of our trust in you to deliver us from every danger and harm. God of grace:
C: *Have mercy on us.*

P: Jesus our great high priest: We are most grateful that in our weaknesses you sympathize with us, since you have been tested like us and suffered like us, but were without sin. Trusting that you do not judge and condemn us, we are confident that we can come to you in prayer, boldly seeking and receiving your grace and mercy in our times of need. God of grace:

Praying the Lectionary

C: *Have mercy on us.*

P: Jesus our loving Savior: You teach us today that people, including us, can fall away from you and your kingdom by being rich in material possessions, yet spiritually poor. Grant us your Holy Spirit's gifts and fruit that we may be generous in sharing our material wealth with the poor, that we may become rich spiritually by trusting in you and following you wherever you lead us. God of grace:
C: *Have mercy on us.*

(Additional prayers may be offered here, ending with: God of grace: **C:** *Have mercy on us.*)

P: Healing Lord: Today we remember all among us who are ill in body, mind or spirit, as well as the widows, widowers, orphans, the unemployed and underemployed, the hungry, homeless and naked, those in prison, the dying and those who have lost loved ones and especially those who we name before you now either aloud or in the silence of our hearts: (NAMES.) God of grace:
C: *Have mercy on us.*

P: God of Israel and the Gentiles: Bestow your Spirit upon the leaders of every nation, that they may govern their peoples with a deep commitment to justice and peace, as well as establish and maintain freedom and democracy for everyone. God of grace:
C: *Have mercy on us.*

P: Lord of the church: Grant unity and goodwill among all Christians and churches, that together we may bear faith-

Praying the Lectionary

ful witness to your gospel in thought, word, and deed. God of grace:
C: *Have mercy on us.*

P: Into your hands we commend all for whom we pray, trusting in your all-sufficient grace; in Jesus' precious name.
ALL: *Amen.*

Pentecost 21

Readings: Job 38:1-7 (38-41); Psalm 104:1-9, 24, 35b; Hebrews 5:1-10; Mark 10:35-45

P: Ancient of days: We praise and thank you for all that you have created and for sustaining life from day to day. You provide the needs of every living creature. Help us to respect your creation, that we may be wise and caring stewards. God of mercy:
C: *Hear our prayer.*

P: Blessed Creator: You are clothed with honor and majesty, wrapped in light as with a garment. How manifold are your works! In wisdom you have made them all; in awe and wonder, we worship you and bless you. God of mercy:
C: *Hear our prayer.*

P: Christ our perfect high priest: We are most grateful that you are the source of eternal salvation for all who obey you. You have made the ultimate sacrifice for our sins and offer us forgiveness. God of mercy:
C: *Hear our prayer.*

P: Jesus, servant of all: Long ago, James and John came to you with a request to be honored by sitting at your right and left hand in your glory. You taught them, and you teach us that true honor and greatness is in serving others. Bestow on us your grace that we may learn from your perfect example how to serve others. God of mercy:

Praying the Lectionary

C: *Hear our prayer.*

(Additional intercessions and thanksgivings may be included here, ending with: God of mercy: **C:** *Hear our prayer.*)

P: Jesus our great physician: We turn to you for healing, and we pray for all among us who are ill in body, mind or spirit, especially: (NAMES.) God of mercy:
C: *Hear our prayer.*

P: God of Israel and the Gentiles: Pour out your grace on the leaders of every nation, including Elizabeth our Queen, our Prime Minister and Members of Parliament, our Premier and Members of the Legislative Assembly, (or other appropriate government leaders and titles for other nations may be added here) that they may govern to establish, protect and maintain the basic rights and freedoms of every citizen, especially those who are voiceless and powerless. God of mercy:
C: *Hear our prayer.*

P: LORD of the church: We pray for unity and goodwill among all Christians around the world; we remember our brothers and sisters in Christ who are wrongfully persecuted, tortured and imprisoned, defend and uphold them in their faith. God of mercy:
C: *Hear our prayer.*

P: In your mercy hear our prayers, O God, Father, Son and Holy Spirit, as you live and reign, one God; now and forever.
ALL: *Amen.*

Pentecost 22

Readings: Job 42:1-6, 10-17; Psalm 34:1-8, (19-22); Hebrews 7:23-28; Mark 10:46-52

P: Holy, blessed Lord God: We praise and thank you for your power to restore the fortunes of those who have endured many sufferings and place their trust in you with repentant hearts. We come to you, like Job with hearts of repentance, trusting in your life-restoring grace and forgiveness. Loving God:
C: *Have mercy on us.*

P: God our redeemer: We bless you, for you deliver us from all our fears; happy are those who take refuge in you. You hear the cries of the poor and save them from troubles. No one who takes refuge in you will be condemned. Loving God:
C: *Have mercy on us.*

P: Christ our perfect high priest: We are most grateful that you are able for all time to save those who approach God through you, since you always live to make intercession for us. You have made the once, all perfect sacrifice, for all time and people by offering your son, as he died on the cross for the sins of the world. Loving God:
C: *Have mercy on us.*

P: Jesus our light: You healed the blind Bartimaeus when he persistently poured out his request to you. May we also be as persistent and urgent in making our requests known

Praying the Lectionary

to you, and thus be healed of our many forms of blindness. Loving God:
C: *Have mercy on us.*

(Other intercessions and thanksgivings may be included here, ending with: Loving God: **C:** *Have mercy on us.*)

P: God of justice and peace: Grant justice and peace to the people and leaders of this nation and every nation on earth. May the free-flowing activity of your Spirit give healing, guidance and grace to all people; especially today we pray for the following persons who are ill in body, mind or spirit: (NAMES.) Loving God:
C: *Have mercy on us.*

P: Merciful Savior: We pray for all Christians around the globe, grant them the riches of your grace and the gifts and fruit of your Holy Spirit, that they may live in love and unity with one another and bear faithful witness to you and your gospel in the world. Loving God:
C: *Have mercy on us.*

P: Hear our prayers Jesus, and give us the faith of Bartimaeus, that we may obediently, freely and joyfully follow wherever you lead us; in your holy name we pray.
ALL: *Amen.*

Reformation Sunday

Readings: Jeremiah 31:31-34; Psalm 46; Romans 3:19-28; John 8:31-36

P: Covenant-making God: We praise and thank you for making a new covenant, written on our hearts. This new covenant makes it possible for everyone to know you, for you forgive and no longer remember our sins. Gracious God:
C: *Hear our prayer.*

P: God our refuge and strength: You are always present to help us in times of trouble. Therefore, we do not have to live our lives in fear. You have the power to make wars cease and rule the earth with your peace. Gracious God:
C: *Hear our prayer.*

P: Righteous God: We confess that it is very difficult to live by Christ's righteousness alone and be justified by his free gift of grace through faith. We find it much easier to live by the law; we are often too strict, rigid and critical in our thoughts, words and actions, we seek to justify ourselves instead of trusting in Jesus Christ to justify us. Forgive us, O Christ: grant us a deeper, richer understanding of our great heritage, that we may truly be enabled and inspired to live by your free and all-sufficient gift of grace. Gracious God:
C: *Hear our prayer.*

Praying the Lectionary

P: Jesus our truth: You have promised that if we abide in your word, you will set us free. May we, with your Spirit's presence, always continue in your word and live in true freedom. Gracious God:
C: *Hear our prayer.*
(Other prayers may be added here, ending with: Gracious God: **C:** *Hear our prayer.*)

P: Ruler of all nations: Bestow your Spirit's gifts and fruit upon Elizabeth our Queen, our Prime Minister and Members of Parliament, our Premier and Members of the Legislative Assembly, (or other appropriate government leaders and titles for other nations may be added here) and the governments of every land, that they may protect and serve the poor and most vulnerable in their midst and govern justly and peacefully. Gracious God:
C: *Hear our prayer.*

P: Lord of the church: We pray that your church would always be in the process of reforming; that the truth of your gospel may take root in every generation and wing its way to every nation. Gracious God:
C: *Hear our prayer.*

P: We ask this in the name of Jesus our reformer and Savior.
ALL: *Amen.*

All Saints' Sunday

Readings: Isaiah 25:6-9 or Wisdom of Solomon 3:1-9; Psalm 24; Revelation 21:1-6a; John 11:32-44

P: Lord of hosts: We praise and thank you for your generosity by providing for all peoples a future and lavish banquet feast. We look forward with hope to celebrate at this heavenly banquet with you, as you destroy death once and forever. At that time, you will wipe away the tears from all of our faces and we, your righteous people, shall live with you in everlasting peace and joy. Merciful God:
C: *Hear our prayer.*

P: King of glory: You are strong and mighty; the earth and all that is in it belongs to you. Grant us clean hands and pure hearts, bless and vindicate us that we may worship, love and serve you all of our days. Merciful God:
C: *Hear our prayer.*

P: God of all things new: We bow in awe and wonder; we are filled with hope and joy as we are given a glimpse into the vision of our future in the last book of the Bible. You shall create a new heaven, a new earth and a new Jerusalem, coming down from heaven. We praise and thank you that in your newness, death will be no more, mourning and crying and pain will be no more; you have won the final victory. Merciful God:
C: *Hear our prayer.*

P: Christ our resurrection and life: Long ago you prepared

Praying the Lectionary

all people of faith for a life of resurrection by raising your friend Lazarus from the dead, as a sign to us that you have the power to destroy death and give new life. For this we are most grateful, and we ask you to help us live under this power of your resurrection life. Show us the signs of resurrection life at work among us today. Merciful God:
C: *Hear our prayer.*

(Additional prayers may be offered here, ending with: Merciful God: **C:** *Hear our prayer.*)

P: Healing Lord: Today we remember all among us who are ill in mind, body, or soul, especially: (NAMES.) Grant them your healing. Merciful God:
C: *Hear our prayer.*

P: Sovereign king: Rule over the hearts and minds of all governments of every land, including: Elizabeth our Queen, our Prime Minister and Members of Parliament, our Premier and Members of the Legislative Assembly, (or other appropriate government leaders and titles for other nations may be added here) that they would govern with justice and work for and maintain peace for all of their citizens. Merciful God:
C: *Hear our prayer.*

P: Christ head of the church: Grace all pastors, bishops, chaplains and laity with the gifts and fruit of your Holy Spirit, that they may live together in unity as they share your love and the gospel with a needy world. Merciful God:
C: *Hear our prayer.*

Praying the Lectionary

P: Hear our prayers, as we commend them into your tender loving care O God, our Father, Son, and Holy Spirit, as you live and reign now and through all ages of ages.
ALL: *Amen.*

Pentecost 23

Readings: Ruth 1:1-18; Psalm 146; Hebrews 9:11-14; Mark 12:28-34

P: God of Naomi and Ruth, and of all peoples: We praise and thank you for your care and protection of the widows Naomi and Ruth. We also thank you for the example of faithfulness of your servant Ruth, who remained with her mother-in-law Naomi. We ask that you also care for and protect all of today's widows and widowers. Compassionate God:
C: *Hear our prayer.*

P: God of heaven and earth: Happy are those whose help and hope is in you, O Lord. You are faithful and execute justice for the oppressed; you give food to the hungry. You set the prisoners free, you open the eyes of the blind; you lift up those who are bowed down; you watch over strangers and uphold orphans, widows and widowers. We pray that you would continue to act in these ways among us today and we are most thankful for your saving work. Compassionate God:
C: *Hear our prayer.*

P: Christ our high priest: We praise and thank you once, for all people and all time obtained our eternal redemption by the shedding of your blood as a perfect sacrifice that purifies our conscience from dead works to worship the living God. Compassionate God:
C: *Hear our prayer.*

Praying the Lectionary

P: Jesus our greatest teacher: Long ago, a scribe asked you which is the greatest of all the commandments. You answered by teaching him that the Lord God of Israel is one and we shall love him with all of our heart, all of our soul, all of our mind, and with all of our strength, and to love our neighbor as ourselves. We are most grateful that the life you lived is our perfect example of how to live this first and greatest commandment; grant us grace to follow you. Compassionate God:
C: *Hear our prayer.*

(Additional thanksgivings and intercessions may be included here, ending with: Compassionate God: **C:** *Hear our prayer.*)

P: Merciful Savior: We turn to you for healing of body, mind and spirit. Please grant your healing to all those who suffer from diseases, handicaps, depression, addictions, abuse, and all other illnesses; we also pray for the dying and those who are mourning the loss of their loved ones, especially: (NAMES.) Compassionate God:
C: *Hear our prayer.*

P: God of all nations: Pour out your wisdom and counsel onto all the leaders of nations, that they would govern to preserve the common good for all their citizens, and that justice and peace would prevail. Compassionate God:
C: *Hear our prayer.*

P: LORD of the church: Grant unity and peace among all Christians and churches, keep those who are persecuted strong in their faith; remember those who are poor and

Praying the Lectionary

forgotten and provide for their needs; bless and prosper the preaching of the gospel in thought, word, and deed that all may know your saving power and love. Compassionate God:
C: *Hear our prayer.*

P: Into your hands gracious God, we commend all for whom we pray, trusting in your mercy through Jesus Christ, our Savior and Lord; who lives and reigns with you and the Holy Spirit; one God, now and forever.
ALL: *Amen.*

Pentecost 24

Readings: Ruth 3:1-5; 4:13-17; Psalm 127; Hebrews 9:24-28; Mark 12:38-44

P: Life-giving God: We praise and thank you for giving the gift of life to your servants Ruth and Boaz by giving them a son named Obed, who became an ancestor to King David and to Jesus. God of mercy:
C: *Hear our prayer.*

P: Lord God: You are the true builder of every house, city and nation; to build without you is to build in vain. Shower us with your grace, that we may always rely on you in everything that we do. God of mercy:
C: *Hear our prayer.*

P: Christ our perfect high priest: We are filled with gratitude for we do not have to endlessly offer imperfect services in order to be forgiven for our sins. Rather, you appeared once for all at the end of the age to remove sin by your sacrificial death on the cross. God of mercy:
C: *Hear our prayer.*

P: Jesus, lover of the poor: You have taught us that the true meaning of generous giving by praising the giving of a poor widow, who put in more than those who gave out of their wealth. By giving out of her poverty, she gave all she had to live on. May we too be generous in our giving and thankful for your abundant provision of us. God of mercy:
C: *Hear our prayer.*

Praying the Lectionary

(Other prayers may be added here, ending with: God of mercy: **C:** *Hear our prayer.*)

P: Healing Savior: We pray for all among us who are ill in mind, body or spirit, that we name aloud or in the silence of our hearts: (PAUSE), especially we remember: (NAMES.) God of mercy:
C: *Hear our prayer.*

P: Heavenly king: Rule over and bestow your grace and wisdom on all the governments of every nation, especially Elizabeth our Queen, our Prime Minister and Members of Parliament, our Premier and Members of the Legislative Assembly, (or other appropriate government leaders and titles for other nations may be added here) and the mayor and city council, that they may administer justice and peace and protect those most vulnerable. God of mercy:
C: *Hear our prayer.*

P: Jesus our Master: Grant your spirit of peace, goodwill and unity among all Christians, that your mission may be accomplished here at home and around the world. God of mercy:
C: *Hear our prayer.*

P: Hear our prayer, and grant whatever else may be in accord with your holy will and purposes, in Jesus' name we pray.
ALL: *Amen.*

Pentecost 25

Readings: 1 Samuel 1:4-20; 1 Samuel 2:1-10; Psalm 16; Hebrews 10:11-14 (15-18) 19-25; Mark 13:1-8

P: God of mercy: We praise and thank you that you listened to and answered the prayers of Hannah by giving her son Samuel, who was consecrated to serve you. We also thank you for listening to our prayers and answering them. Gracious God:
C: *Have mercy, and hear us.*

P: Holy One: There is no one besides you; you are our rock. You raise the poor from the dust and the needy from the ash heap, to make them sit with noble ones and inherit a seat of honor. We thank you for guarding the feet of your faithful ones. Gracious God:
C: *Have mercy, and hear us.*

P: God our refuge: We ask for your protection throughout our life-journey. You are our chosen portion and our cup; you hold our lot. We bless you for giving us counsel and instruction by showing us the path of life. Gracious God:
C: *Have mercy, and hear us.*

P: Jesus our new and living way: We praise and thank you for giving us access to God by your once, perfect sacrifice, for all time and peoples through which we receive the forgiveness of sin. You have given us hope for the future so that we can provoke one another to love and good deeds,

Praying the Lectionary

encouraging one another, and all the more as we see the day approaching. Gracious God:
C: *Have mercy and hear us.*

P: Christ our alpha and omega: You predicted the destruction of the Jerusalem temple as well as signs that would usher in the end times. You have warned us of false messiahs, wars and rumors of wars, of nation rising against nation, and kingdom against kingdom; of natural disasters; all of which are signs of the beginning of birth pangs. As we face the uncertainties of the future, grant us a deep trust in you, knowing that our eternal security rests in you. Gracious God:
C: *Have mercy, and hear us.*

(Other intercessions and thanksgivings may be added here, ending with: Gracious God: **C:** *Have mercy, and hear us.*)

P: Healing Messiah: We remember all among us who are ill in body, mind or spirit, especially: (NAMES.) Gracious God:
C: *Have mercy, and hear us.*

P: God of heaven and earth: Shower your grace and wisdom on all the leaders of nations, especially Elizabeth our Queen, our Prime Minister and Members of Parliament, our Premier and Members of the Legislative Assembly, (or other appropriate government leaders and titles for other nations may be added here) our mayor and city councilors, that they may govern responsibly and utilize their authority for the common good of everyone and especially

Praying the Lectionary

protect the interests of the poorest and most vulnerable in their midst. Gracious God:
C: *Have mercy and hear us.*

P: Blessed Savior: You love your church and have provided it with the perfect example of how we are to love one another and spread that love into every corner of the globe. Bestow your Holy Spirit's gifts and fruit, that all Christians might live in unity with one another and bear witness to you and the gospel. Gracious God:
C: *Have mercy and hear us.*
P: Hear our prayer, O Triune God, and grant all other things that may be in accord with your holy will and purposes; we pray this in the holy name of Jesus.
ALL: *Amen.*

Christ The King Sunday

Readings: 2 Samuel 23:1-7; Psalm 132:1-12 [13-18]; Revelations 1:4b-8; John 18:33-37

P: Strong one of Israel: We praise and thank you for ruling over your people with justice; your Spirit is like the light of morning, the sun rising on a cloudless day, gleaming from the rain on the grassy land. Remember and bless all political leaders, as you remembered and blessed David of old. King of kings:
C: *Hear our prayer.*

P: Gracious ruler: You promised your servant David that one day in the future, through his line the Messiah-king would be born and rule Israel and all peoples. In Zion he shall reign and abundantly bless the people, satisfying the poor with bread; clothing the priests with righteousness; and giving joy to the faithful. Today we look forward with hope and deep longing for your rule, Jesus our Messiah-king. King of kings:
C: *Hear our prayer.*

P: Exalted Christ: You are creation's Lord over the past, present and future. We are most thankful for the grace, peace, love, and freedom that are ours as subjects of your wonderful dominion. King of kings:
C: *Hear our prayer.*

P: Author of truth: We confess that even as subjects of your kingdom, we have resisted and thwarted your reign

in our hearts, souls, minds, and lives. We have been reluctant to share your gospel kingdom with the sick, the lonely, depressed, and others whom we know are in need. Forgive us and help us to be more willing, faithful servants. As your forgiven followers, we now pray for healing for those who are ill in mind, body or spirit, especially: (NAMES.) King of kings:
C: *Hear our prayer.*

(Additional prayers may be offered here, ending with: King of kings: **C:** *Hear our prayer.*)

P: Leader of all nations: Bestow the treasures of your counselor, the Spirit, upon the leaders of church and state. Assist them in the exercise of discernment, tolerance, kindness, and love. Aid people of every nation to accept one another as brothers and sisters and strive for peace and justice in this world. King of kings:
C: *Hear our prayer.*

P: Christ our king: May your Lordship so permeate our being, that in every area of our living we may be subjects of your gracious leading, now and always, as we pray the prayer your taught us:
ALL: *Our Father... Amen.*

Thanksgiving Sunday

Readings: Joel 2:21-27; Psalm 126; 1 Timothy 2:1-7; Matthew 6:25-33

P: Most generous God: Today we praise and thank you for the legacy of your abundant provision. Long ago you blessed your chosen people and their land by providing fertile soil, green pastures, and bountiful harvests of figs, grapes, wine, grain, and oil. So down through the centuries you have also blessed the earth, and sustained it with abundant life, in order that people of every land my turn to you for life, health, and salvation. Thank you, God:
C: *Hear our prayer.*

P: Most generous God: When the Lord restored the fortunes of Zion, your people were like those who dream. Their mouths were filled with laughter, and their tongues with shouts of joy, for the Lord had done great things for them, and they rejoiced. May those who sow in tears reap with shouts of joy as you deliver them and provide for all of their needs. Thank you, God:
C: *Hear our prayer.*

P: Most generous God: You are worthy to be worshipped and served with Christians of every generation, may we be faithful in offering supplications, prayers, intercessions, and thanksgiving for everyone, including the leaders of all nations, that we may lead a quiet and peaceable life in all godliness and dignity. Thank you, God:
C: *Hear our prayer.*

Praying the Lectionary

P: Most generous God: Your son Jesus taught us not to worry about our life, what we will eat or what we will drink, or about our body, what we will wear. Help us to remember that life is more than food, and the body is more than clothing. We are of more value than the birds of the air and yet you provide for them. The lilies of the field are clothed with their beauty by you, and how much more shall you provide for and clothe us. Instead of worrying about these things, help us to strive first for the kingdom of God and his righteousness, and all these things will be given to us as well. Thank you, God:
C: *Hear our prayer.*

(Other intercessions and thanksgivings may be included here, ending with: Thank you God: **C:** *Hear our prayer.*)

P: Most generous God: You are the healer of us all, so we uphold before you now all among us who are ill in body, mind or soul, especially: (NAMES.) Grant them your healing presence and grace. Thank you, God:
C: *Hear our prayer.*

P: Most generous God: We take a moment to offer you our thanks for whatever else may come to mind, or be on our hearts, or that we so often take for granted, we bring them before you in silence now: (PAUSE.) Thank you, God:
C: *Hear our prayer.*

P: Most generous God: We pray for your church around the globe; bless all bishops, pastors, and chaplains with your grace that they may faithfully lead your people to

Praying the Lectionary

walk in your ways and share your love with the world's most needy. Thank you, God:
C: *Hear our prayer.*

P: Hear our prayers and grant whatever else may serve your holy will and purposes, O God; for the sake of your son, Christ our Savior and Lord, who lives and reigns with you and the Holy Spirit, one God; now and forever.
ALL: *Amen.*

Praying the Lectionary

GARTH WEHRFRITZ-HANSON attended and received his Bachelor of Arts degree from the University of Saskatchewan, Saskatoon, and his Master of Divinity degree from Lutheran Theological Seminary in Saskatoon, Saskatchewan, Canada. A recently retired ordained pastor in the Evangelical Lutheran Church in Canada, he has served several congregations in the Alberta and the Territories Synod. He also served as a chaplain in the Good Samaritan Society facility of South Ridge Village in Medicine Hat, Alberta, and as chaplain with the Bethany Group in Camrose, Alberta. He is married to Julianna, also a Lutheran pastor. Reverend Wehrfritz-Hanson is the author of *Praying The Lectionary Prayers Of The Church Cycle A*, also published by CSS. He enjoys hiking, bicycling, cross-country skiing, reading and amateur photography, and continues to serve as a pulpit supply pastor.